Plan & Go: Lone Star Hiking Trail

All you need to know to complete Texas' longest wilderness footpath

Kevin Muschter

sandiburg press

Plan & Go: Lone Star Hiking Trail

All you need to know to complete Texas' longest wilderness footpath

Copyright © 2015 by Kevin Muschter and sandiburg press

ISBN 978-1-943126-01-9

Front and back cover photos copyright © 2015 by Kevin Muschter
Unless otherwise stated, all interior photos by Kevin Muschter

Editor: Gerret Kalkoffen

Published by sandiburg press
www.sandiburgpress.com

Cover photos: Double Lake Recreation Area (front); Double Lake Branch (back)

Content

Welcome

This book was written to provide all the necessary information to thoroughly prepare and successfully complete a hike on the Lone Star Hiking Trail (commonly abbreviated as "LSHT"). Regardless of whether you intend to walk Texas' longest wilderness footpath from end to end or in sections, I am confident you will be well-equipped and save valuable time and effort on planning if you use the information and advice compiled in this guide.

The following chapters contain essential hiking information, such as trail conditions, camping choices, and gear recommendations, to help you weigh up options and create a hiking itinerary that meets your personal preferences and abilities. You will also find practical advice regarding travel arrangements, meal preparation, and training along with a brief overview of the trail's history and flora & fauna. No matter whether you are still toying with the idea of hiking the LSHT or have already decided to embark on this adventure, I hope this book will be a helpful resource and source of inspiration.

The large number of animal species and abundant vegetation along the LSHT make for a great wilderness adventure in one of the most biodiverse areas in the United States. You will be surrounded by enormous pine trees, pass through extensive palmetto swamps, and cross a multitude of creeks and streams meandering through the Sam Houston National Forest. Weather conditions will be pleasant from late fall to early spring. Taking some time off to experience the solitude and nature's beauty along this route through East Texas wilderness is absolutely worth it. Without a doubt, completing the LSHT will be a rewarding accomplishment and memorable experience in your life.

Western Terminus of the LSHT near Richards, TX

1. Introduction

The Lone Star Hiking Trail is a 96.5-mile footpath in Texas, located about an hour north of Houston in the Sam Houston National Forest. With a cumulative length of 128 miles, including the main trail plus over 30 miles of additional loop and crossover trails, it is the longest continuously marked and maintained path in the Lone Star State. The main route connects the Western Terminus near Richards and the Eastern Terminus near Cleveland. The LSHT can be hiked in both directions and it will take the average hiker between six and ten days to complete. The shaded and secluded trail is open year-round and known for its immense biodiversity. Its beautiful forest setting and rich wildlife invite outdoor enthusiasts of all ages and fitness levels, whether it is just for a day hike or a weeklong backpacking trip.

The idea of establishing a hiking trail through East Texas wilderness with ample camping opportunities was first introduced by members of the Lone Star Chapter of the Sierra Club in 1966. Their proposal of a 100-mile nature path through the Sam Houston National Forest was approved by the U. S. Forest Service and work began in 1967. Much of the marking and construction of the LSHT was done by the Sierra Club and many other volunteers under the sponsorship of the U. S. Forest Service. The main trail was completed and turned over to forest authorities in 1972. An extension to the LSHT, consisting of several loop and crossover trails, was approved later and completed in 1978. To this day, maintenance of the 128-mile trail system is largely carried out by non-profit organizations, such as the Lone Star Hiking Trail Club and LSHT Conservancy, who dedicate many hours of volunteer labor each year.

My personal LSHT adventure began in November 2014 while I was researching options for a possible long-distance hiking trip to take place in early 2015. Since many of the alpine trails are usually buried under feet-high snow during the late winter/early spring months, I was looking for an alternative route that would provide an adequate challenge, reasonable trail and weather conditions, and not require any special gear or permits.

The LSHT seemed to offer all of that and much more. When I learned about the special characteristics of the trail, the abundant wildlife and vegetation in the Sam Houston National Forest, and the more favorable climate during the winter months, my decision was made. Plus, I had never been to East Texas before, so this was an excellent opportunity to go on a great hike and get to know another unique region of the United States.

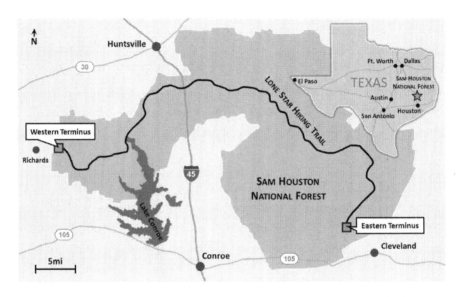

Figure 1 – Overview Map of the Lone Star Hiking Trail

Summarizing my own experience and research, this book was written to provide a clear picture of what to expect of the LSHT, to encourage others to venture out and experience this hidden gem of Texas for themselves, and to provide a comprehensive and practical guide that will enable future LSHT hikers to confidently plan and efficiently prepare their own adventure. *Chapter 2* summarizes the challenge at hand in terms of physical and technical requirements and it also provides tools to estimate the time and budget needed. *Chapter 3* gives an overview of trail and weather conditions to be expected, points of interest along the route, camping options, water availability, safety notes, as well as animal and plant life. *Chapter 4* discusses trip planning items that generally warrant sufficient lead time, not only to potentially save money, but also to ensure that preferred options are available. *Chapter 5* covers specific details on itinerary planning, proper training, and nutrition to help you carefully and effectively prepare your own trip. *Chapter 6* provides an overview of essential hiking gear items together with LSHT-specific advice to support your decision on what gear to obtain and to carry along. Lastly, *Chapter 7* summarizes all efforts and considerations that went into my own 6-day journey on the LSHT in February 2015. These personal accounts are intended to provide inspiration, guidance, and additional reference points. Ultimately, I hope you will find this book to be a valuable resource for shaping your own adventure on Texas' longest wilderness footpath.

Happy Trails!

Visit *www.PlanAndGoHiking.com* for more information and pictures.

2. Summary of the Challenge

Can you hike the LSHT? If you are genuinely interested in hiking and have some experience, the answer is most definitely yes! However, the trail does not come without its own challenges. This chapter gives a brief summary of what is required from a physical and technical perspective, how much time should be allotted, and which financial implications to take into consideration.

a. Requirements

Walking the 96.5 miles of the LSHT is a moderately difficult challenge, suitable even for outdoor enthusiasts with little or no thru-hiking experience. A decent level of fitness is certainly advisable, and hikers should possess the ability to carry the additional weight of their gear and supplies over the full distance.

From a technical perspective, the trail profile is rather flat without any of the difficulties hikers are usually faced with in more alpine regions, such as high altitude and steep slopes. However, the trail is crossed by a multitude of rivers and creeks and stable bridges are not always available. In cases where there is no bridge, you will be required to either ford the stream or cross on potentially slippery logs. There are also muddy sections along the trail that require a certain level of surefootedness when traversing.

Additional requirements include the ability to quickly adjust to changing weather conditions (intermittent showers can occur at any given time) and being able to endure hot temperatures and high humidity levels (especially during summer). You should also be prepared to cope with all the constraints associated with camping out in nature, e.g., preparing food with limited resources, sleeping in a shelter with minimal comfort, and not having the luxury of a private bathroom.

b. Time

Walking the entire length of the LSHT at an average pace usually takes between eight and ten days. Very fit, experienced hikers may be able to complete the full distance in as little as four to five days.

Estimating your days on the trail is the first step in planning your own LSHT adventure. Figure 2 is intended to provide guidance for an initial assessment. Selecting your age and corresponding fitness level will give you an idea of how long it will approximately take you to complete the trail.[1] For example, a 40-year-old person with an average fitness level can expect to spend roughly eight days on the trail.

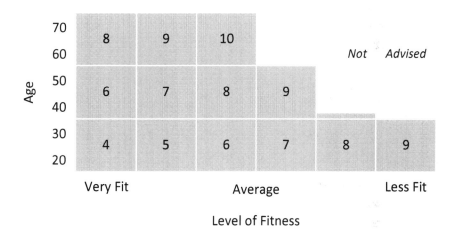

Figure 2 – Estimate of Trail Days on the LSHT

Once you have determined your estimate of trail days (ETD), you can calculate your average daily mileage by dividing the total distance of the LSHT by your ETD:

Average miles per day = 96 miles / ETD

---

[1] Numbers based on personal estimate and feedback from fellow LSHT hikers.

Continuing the above example leads to an average of 96/8 = 12 miles per day. While this is a good initial estimate, additional factors need to be taken into consideration as they may affect your total ETD.

During my hike on the LSHT, I met a couple (in their late 50s) who were planning on spending ten days for hiking and two additional days for exploring the recreational opportunities along the trail. Another thru-hiker I met (in his mid-40s) was not on a particular schedule and told me "it will take as long as it takes".

In order to account for individual preferences and available time, consider the following questions to further personalize your itinerary:

Do you plan to resupply along the trail?

People who plan to thru-hike the LSHT in a week or less may choose not to resupply food during their trip. However, if your hiking strategy provides for resupplying at some point during the trip, this may require spending some time off the trail.

- If you plan to resupply off the trail, add 0.5 to 1 day to your ETD depending on your resupply location

What weather conditions are to be expected?

It is not uncommon for weather conditions to change quickly in Texas. Seasonal thunderstorms and torrential downpours may force you to leave the trail for an extended period of time to seek a safe shelter in a nearby settlement. While this is certainly difficult to predict at the time of planning your trip, you may want to include an additional cushion in your ETD to account for unfavorable weather conditions.

- If there is a high chance of severe weather conditions to occur (e.g., if you are traveling during summer months), add 0.5 to 1 day to your ETD

Would you like to include additional time for relaxing along the trail or for exploring nearby recreational areas?

The LSHT offers many opportunities for relaxing and additional exploring. Huntsville State Park and Double Lake Recreation Area are popular examples for zero days[2]. Section 3b *Points of Interest* covers these and other options in more detail.

- If you plan on relaxing/exploring along the trail, add the respective number of zero days to your ETD

With your initial ETD from Figure 2 and the additional days resulting from the above questions, calculate your total days on the trail. In our example, the 40-year-old hiker chooses to add three days to the initial ETD: half a day for resupplying, half a day for poor weather conditions, and two zero days for exploring Huntsville State Park and Double Lake Recreation Area. This leads to a total estimate of 11 trail days.

The resulting total ETD should be the basis for all your subsequent planning regarding travel, food, and resupply. If you cannot answer these questions just yet, don't worry. You may only know whether or not you would like to spend more time in certain areas after further research. You can always update your estimate later on.

c. Budget

Walking the LSHT is a rather budget-friendly endeavor. It doesn't require the purchase of permits, and camping in primitive hiker or hunter camps along the trail is free. However, staying at one of the designated campgrounds will incur a fee; between $15 and $27 per night.

If you don't live close to the trail or even outside of the United States, travel-related expenses will likely represent the largest portion of the required budget. Factors to consider are the airfare to Houston, gasoline costs if you decide to drive, expenses for accommodation (before and after the trip), and costs for transportation to and from the trailheads. A taxi, for example, will cost approximately $2.25 per mile.

---

[2] Days on which no or no significant hiking occurs; typically used to recover.

If this is your first multi-day hiking trip, you may also want to factor in the costs of assembling the necessary gear. Regardless of whether you choose to buy or rent, it is highly recommended to opt for good quality equipment. Functionality and durability are important factors when choosing the right gear along with comfort level and weight. Going with the cheapest option just to save a few dollars is not advised. You may regret your decision later on when you have to fix a broken shoulder strap halfway through your trip or deal with water dripping on your face at night because the top of your tent has a leak. Depending on your specific needs and preferences, the expenses for buying a basic kit of decent quality equipment will likely range anywhere from $800 to $1000. For an overview of basic hiking gear items and options as well as LSHT-specific recommendations refer to Chapter 6 *Gear*. Those interested in renting gear should check with their local outfitter to find out more about available options and related costs.

By comparison, buying the necessary food supplies for your trip will represent a relatively small portion of the budget. Freeze-dried meals are very convenient but certainly more expensive (ca. $7-10 per meal) than home-made meals. Refer to Section 5c *Food* for related considerations and suggested meal plans. Additional costs may be incurred if you choose to utilize resupply services. See Section 5d *Resupply* for available options along the LSHT.

3. What to Expect

This chapter gives you a comprehensive overview of what to look forward to and what to look out for when attempting to thru-hike the LSHT. The information provided will assist you in choosing appropriate gear and creating a schedule that suits your personal preferences and abilities.

a. Trails & Navigation

The LSHT is a foot travel only trail. Motorized vehicles, bicycles, horses, and equipment of any kind are prohibited. Hiking conditions are easy to moderate and basic navigating skills are generally sufficient.

Trail Conditions

Meandering the breadth of the Sam Houston National Forest, the LSHT and its side trails follow a relatively flat terrain through beautiful biodiverse scenery. Elevation ranges from 150 to 400 feet above sea level without any major ascents or descents. Towering trees provide plenty of shade and protection from wind and rain.

Creeks, rivers, and extensive wetlands pose the main challenge along the trail. While a number of bridges and boardwalks have been installed to allow for easy crossing, they occasionally get damaged or destroyed during flooding. Many of the streams are usually dry or low on water, but crossing can still be challenging at times as some of the river beds are up to 10 feet deep. Be prepared to scramble down and up a few steep banks in order to get to the other side.

Throughout the forest, soil conditions vary from dry, sandy uplands to muddy bottomlands. Heavy rain can change conditions quickly, making certain sections of the trail trickier to cross. Watch out for slippery logs or slopes and expect to get your feet wet occasionally. This particularly holds true for crossing the spillway near Camelia Lake (mile 32.0) and fording the East Fork of the San Jacinto River (mile 71.1). Fallen trees and overgrowth may pose further obstacles along the trail but are usually of non-permanent nature.

The LSHT is primarily a path through pristine nature with only a few sections following service and public roads. Gravel and asphalt are predominant surfaces there. When walking along roads or highways, expect to be more directly exposed to sun light, wind, and rain as there are fewer trees to provide protection.

Navigation

The route of the LSHT and its side trails is continuously marked in both directions. There are trail markers at regular intervals, mile markers at nearly every full mile, and additional sign posts at main intersections of the trail.

Figure 3 – Regular Trail Markers and Sign Post

The main trail is marked with unpainted 2x4-inch metal plates nailed on trees and posts, usually within sight distance of one another. Tilted trail markers indicate turns and the direction of the turn. Double trail markers indicate sharp turns or areas where hikers needs to pay particular attention to the route. Loop or crossover trails of the LSHT are marked with horizontally striped metal plates. Each side trail has a different color stripe (see Appendix E for details).

Figure 4 – Tilted Double Trail Markers and Side Trail Marker

Nearly every full mile of the trail is marked with a mile marker indicating the distance traveled from the Western Terminus to the Eastern Terminus. Newer mile markers are metal or plastic posts staked in the ground adjacent to the trail. Older mile markers are diamond-shaped red and white metal plates nailed to trees slightly above eye level. Between miles 75 and 96, hikers will notice additional aluminum plates on trees and posts showing a different, declining number. Those mile markers indicate the distance traveled in the opposite direction, from the Eastern Terminus to Double Lake Recreation Area.

Figure 5 – Old and New Mile Markers

Trail and mile markers are generally omitted along public roads and highways. A few markers may also be missing in the woods as a result of fallen trees or vandalism. However, for the majority of the trail you should never walk for more than a few minutes without seeing a trail marker. If you find yourself in a situation like that, you may have wandered off the trail. In order to get back on track, it is best to simply turn around and backtrack your way to the last marker you have seen.

(i) Since the trail is marked in both directions, it can be helpful to also check the backside of trees in front of you in situations where directions may not be 100% clear.

Maps

Large-scale topographic maps are generally not required for navigating on the LSHT due to the clear and continuous marking of the route. Basic overview maps of the area can be downloaded for free from U. S. Forest Service and LSHT Club websites. The U. S. Forest Service publishes a map of the entire Sam Houston National Forest which also includes the route of the LSHT along with available campsite options. The LSHT Club offers a number of maps with additional information. The selection ranges from overview maps to more detailed topographic maps for each trail section.

Note: Certain sections of the trail, in particular those unmarked, can be confusing at times. To help hikers navigate through those areas confidently, the Compact Trail Guide in Appendix B includes detailed directions for all major waypoints. Table 1 below provides a few examples.

Mile	Waypoint
20.3	Trail enters woods to the right (across from Stubblefield overflow camping area), after 300 feet the trail takes a sharp left (watch as there is a trail that goes straight!)
32.0	Turn left onto paved road, follow for a couple hundred feet until you reach a small brick building, walk towards Camelia Lake on left, cross the dam (careful, spillway can be slippery), trail turns right after dam
59.8	Trail intersects gravel road, two options: (1) turn right to continue on LSHT, enter woods after 60 feet to left; (2) turn left and walk 300 feet to get to Big Woods hiker camp

Table 1 – Examples of Waypoints & Directions

Trailheads

Currently, there are 14 trailheads along the LSHT (see Table 2). 13 of which provide direct access to the main trail and an additional one provides access via Little Lake Creek Loop Trail (LLCLT). Trailhead #5 is permanently closed, however, the official numbering has not been adjusted. Therefore, the Eastern Terminus trailhead is still referred to as TH#15.

Mile	Trailhead ID & Name
0.0	TH#1 - Richards
3.5	TH#2 - Sand Branch
8.7	TH#3 - N. Wilderness
LLCLT	TH#4 - Caney Creek
16.0	TH#6 - S. Stubblefield
35.0	TH#7 - Huntsville
45.0	TH#8 - Four Notch
62.8	TH#9 - Big Woods
67.4	TH#10 - Magnolia
73.8	TH#11 - Iron Ore
79.9	TH#12 - Big Creek
82.5	TH#13 - Tarkington
90.9	TH#14 - Mercy Fire Tower
96.5	TH#15 - Winters Bayou

Table 2 – Trailheads of the LSHT

Each trailhead has its own parking area where hikers can park their vehicles free of charge. There are no restroom facilities at any of the parking lots because the trail is intended to be primitive. Hikers should pay particular attention to the trailhead information boards as they may display valuable information for the upcoming trail section. Hikers are also encouraged to register at each trailhead using the drop boxes and sign-in sheets provided. This will help forest authorities determine the number of people on the trail faster in case of emergency.

Trail Sections

Trailheads and other major landmarks can be used to divide the LSHT into smaller subsections. This may be helpful for hikers who prefer to complete the trail in sections rather than as a whole. The sections listed in Table 3 below are commonly used in LSHT resources. While thru-hikers may also find this information useful for their daily trip planning, they need to be aware that camping is prohibited in trailhead parking areas.

Section Name	Length (mi)	Trail Segment
01-Wilderness	8.7	TH#1 to TH#3
02-Kelly	7.3	TH#3 to TH#6
03-Stubblefield	12.8	TH#6 to West Huntsville hiker camp (mile 28.8)
04-Huntsville	6.2	West Huntsville hiker camp (mile 28.8) to TH#7
05-Phelps	10.0	TH#7 to TH#8
06-Four Notch	9.2	TH#8 to Intersection of FS202 & FS207 (mile 54.2)
07-Big Woods	8.6	Intersection of FS202 & FS207 (mile 54.2) to TH#9
08-Magnolia	11.0	TH#9 to TH#11
09-Big Creek	8.7	TH#11 to TH#13
10-Tarkington	8.4	TH#13 to TH#14
11-Winters Bayou	5.6	TH#14 to TH#15

Table 3 – Trail Sections of the LSHT

b. Points of Interest

There are a number of areas along the trail that deserve or require particular attention. Hikers may want to consider incorporating additional time or even zero days in their itineraries for further exploration.

Cagle Recreation Area

Cagle Recreation Area is a campground located along the east shoreline of Lake Conroe. It is a 5.4-mile side trip (there and back) from LSHT mile 16. Cagle offers lakeshore hiking and bicycle trails, wildlife viewing, water sports, fishing, and a picnic area overlooking Lake Conroe. The area is covered with beautiful large pine and hardwood trees plus thousands of colorful wildflowers. Mid-February redbud tree blossoms followed by dogwood tree blossoms in early March are a spectacular outdoor flower show.

Lake Conroe

Lake Conroe lies in the southwest of the Sam Houston National Forest. It is the reserve drinking water supply for the City of Houston. The man-made lake offers 22,000 acres of water-oriented recreation such as fishing, canoeing, and boating. If you decide not to include the Cagle Recreation Area in your itinerary, you will get another excellent view of Lake Conroe at approx. mile 16.5 of the LSHT. The National Forest lands that surround the lake provide the wintering habitat for the endangered bald eagle. During winter months, the majestic bird may be spotted soaring over the lake, perched on a flooded tree stump, or in a tall pine along the shoreline.

Stubblefield Lake Recreation Area

Stubblefield Lake Recreation Area is located on the west side of the Sam Houston National Forest along the north shore of Lake Conroe. Its beautiful quiet forest setting makes for a relaxing outdoor experience. Recreational activities include fishing, hiking, bird-watching, picnicking, and camping. At mile 19.7, the LSHT passes right through the recreation area.

Huntsville State Park

Huntsville State Park is a 4.4-mile side trip (there and back) from LSHT mile 35.7. The park's woodlands are a great environment for camping and other outdoor activities, offering over 25 miles of additional trails for hiking, mountain biking, and horseback riding. There is ample opportunity to study nature and observe wildlife. Huntsville State Park is home to many different birds, including a number of migratory birds at the right time of year. Deer, raccoons, fox squirrels, opossums, and armadillos inhabit the woods. The park surrounds Lake Raven, which allows for a variety of water activities, such as canoeing, fishing, boating, and swimming. While enjoying the lake, visitors may even spot basking turtles and alligators. The park store, called "Gator Junction", sells camping and fishing supplies, groceries, ice cream, cold drinks, ice, souvenirs, and more. The daily park entrance fee is $5 for adults.

San Jacinto River East Fork Crossing

At mile 71.1, hikers will reach the banks of the East Fork of the San Jacinto River. The footbridge, which used to allow hikers to cross the river safely, got destroyed by flooding in 2004. There are plans to replace the bridge in the future. In the meantime, hikers can decide between fording the river and following an unmarked unofficial detour. Fording may be too dangerous or even impossible during high water. Following the approx. 3-mile detour will require advanced navigation skills, a compass and/or GPS device, and forcing your way through 0.2 miles of dense underbrush. Both options bear different challenges and risks, and should therefore be thoroughly evaluated as part of the individual itinerary planning process.

(i) The LSHT Club website (*http://www.lonestartrail.org*) offers current information on the San Jacinto River East Fork detour as well as a detailed map and directions for download.

Double Lake Recreation Area

Double Lake Recreation Area is located on the east side of the Sam Houston National Forest. It surrounds a 24-acre, spring-fed lake and includes whispering pines and hardwoods. Built initially in 1937 by the Civilian Conservation Corps, the facilities of the recreation area include camping sites, picnic tables, swimming area with a beach, and a concession stand with bathhouse. Canoes and paddleboats can be rented at the concession stand at Double Lake which also has snacks, ice, and other items for sale. Bass, bream, and catfish have been stocked in Double Lake, and fishing is permitted under applicable state laws. At mile 75.0, the Double Lake Recreation Area is only a few steps away from the LSHT.

Big Creek Scenic Area

The Big Creek Scenic Area was established in 1962 as a special interest area within the Sam Houston National Forest. It encompasses 1,460 acres of meandering creeks, lush pine-hardwood forest, and varied flora and fauna. The area was set aside primarily for recreational enjoyment, however, camping and campfires are prohibited within the boundaries of the protected area. The LSHT goes through the scenic area (miles 78.6-80.8), offering various trail loops for hikers to enjoy. You could hardly do better than to take a short (or longer) hike along those trails for a chance to see some of the more wary and elusive wildlife creatures of the eastern Texas Piney Woods region, such as armadillos, bobcats, river otters, red-shouldered hawks, and even copperhead snakes.

Table 4 provides an overview of points of interest along the LSHT including mileages to facilitate individual itinerary planning.

Mile	Point of Interest
16.0+2.7[3]	Cagle Recreation Area
16.5	Great view of Lake Conroe
19.7	Stubblefield Lake Recreation Area
35.7+2.2	Huntsville State Park
71.1	San Jacinto River East Fork Crossing
75.0	Double Lake Recreation Area
78.6	Big Creek Scenic Area (2.2-mile section)

Table 4 – Points of Interest

---

[3] Whenever a particular point of interest is located off the main trail, the stated mileage represents the closest LSHT mile plus the one way distance to the POI in miles.

c. Weather

The Sam Houston National Forest has a warm, temperate climate with hot, humid summers and short, mild winters. The region is known for its quickly changing weather conditions. There is even a popular saying:

"If you don't like the weather in Texas, wait five minutes, and it'll change!"

Temperature

The warm season in East Texas usually lasts from May to September. With average daily high temperatures climbing well into the 90s and humidity levels peaking, walking on the LSHT during those months can be particularly strenuous. People attempting a thru-hike during summer are advised to take necessary precautions for extreme heat. Staying well hydrated and walking at a slower pace are highly advisable to prevent overexertion.

Month	Temp. °F (high/low)	Humidity % (high/low)
January	59 / 40	89 / 49
February	63 / 43	90 / 52
March	70 / 49	90 / 49
April	78 / 57	91 / 46
May	85 / 65	91 / 46
June	90 / 71	92 / 48
July	93 / 73	92 / 45
August	94 / 73	91 / 41
September	88 / 68	92 / 43
October	80 / 59	92 / 45
November	69 / 50	91 / 47
December	61 / 41	89 / 48

Sources: US Climate Data, WeatherSpark; Period 1981-2012.

Table 5 – Average Temperatures & Humidity Levels (Huntsville, TX)

Late fall, winter, and early spring are much better seasons for hiking on the LSHT. From November through March, daytime highs usually stay below 70°F. January is typically the coldest month. Be prepared for nighttime temperatures around or even below freezing. Temperatures in October and April are usually still pleasant enough for hiking.

Precipitation

The average rainfall in Sam Houston National Forest amounts to 49 inches per year with a precipitation probability ranging from 27% to 39%. The most common forms of precipitation are thunderstorms, moderate rain, and light rain. The intensity of precipitation varies by season.

During the warm season (May to September), there is a 36% average chance that precipitation will be observed at some point during the day. When it does occur, it is most often in the form of thunderstorms (76% of days with precipitation have at worst thunderstorms), light rain (12%), heavy rain (6%), and moderate rain (6%).

Month	Precip. inch (avg)	Precip. % (avg)	T-Storm % (avg)
January	4.3	33	6
February	3.4	33	8
March	3.7	32	11
April	3.3	29	15
May	4.5	32	21
June	5.4	38	29
July	2.8	39	31
August	3.7	36	28
September	4.2	33	20
October	4.7	27	12
November	5.2	31	10
December	4.1	33	7

Sources: US Climate Data, WeatherSpark; Period 1981-2012.

Table 6 – Average Precipitation (Huntsville, TX)

During the cold season (November to March), there is a 33% average chance that precipitation will be observed at some point during the day. When precipitation does occur, it is most often in the form of light rain (39% of days with precipitation have at worst light rain), thunderstorms

(22%), moderate rain (19%), and heavy rain (16%). Snowfall is not to be expected in East Texas.

While thunderstorms are much more likely during summer, they can occur at any given time throughout the year. Be prepared to react quickly if you see clouds starting to form. Given the high chance of precipitation, it is not recommended to head out on the trail for an extended period of time without proper rain gear. Bring at least a light rain jacket and a rain cover for your backpack and make sure to have both items readily available at the top of your pack.

> **!** When seeking shelter during a thunderstorm, move away from freestanding trees and place your pack and other metal objects at a distance. Open fields and roads should be avoided by all means.

Other Conditions

During the warm season, insects can be particularly bothersome. Flies, ticks, mosquitoes, and chiggers love the hot and humid climate and will claim their share of the Sam Houston National Forest from May to October. During those months, make sure to always carry insect repellent and wear long sleeve shirts and pants. You may even want to consider bringing a mosquito head net for additional protection.

> **!** Keep in mind that taking necessary precautions to minimize contact with insects is not only a matter of comfort, but also advisable to prevent potential exposure to insect-borne diseases, such as Lyme disease.

Tornadoes and hurricanes are part of the seasonal weather phenomena in East Texas. Tornadoes may occur during any month and at any hour of the day. They occur with greatest frequency during late spring and early summer months, between the hours of 4pm and 8pm. While conditions for the possibility of a tornado can be predicted hours before an event, the actual tornado rarely leaves much more than a couple minutes of warning, if any. They usually only last for a few minutes but can cause serious destruction due to the extreme wind speeds, the heavy rain, and strong lightning.

Hurricanes occur less frequently throughout the year with peak season in late summer and fall. They are more predictable than tornadoes. The exact area in which the storm system will hit is usually known several days in advance. Hurricanes last significantly longer and impact a much greater area. Any hurricane hitting the East Texas Gulf Coast is likely to reach far into the inland and affect the Sam Houston National Forest as well, usually in the form of high winds and heavy rainfall.

| ! | Windy conditions may increase the risk of big branches and trees falling. Heavy rain can cause creeks and rivers to quickly rise out of their banks. Always check the weather forecast before venturing onto the LSHT, especially during hurricane peak season.

d. Camping

Hikers can choose from different camping options along the LSHT based on their personal comfort level needs and the overall hiking strategy. There are a few regional and seasonal camping restrictions in Sam Houston National Forest that hikers need to be aware of and pay particular attention to as part of the trip planning process.

Primitive Camping

Primitive camping is permitted anywhere along the LSHT with three exceptions: trailhead parking areas, the protected Big Creek Scenic Area, and private properties. During hunting season, usually late September through early January, camping is further restricted to developed campgrounds, hiker camps, and hunter camps. Campfires are allowed in designated areas, which are usually equipped with fire rings, unless banned completely during dry seasons. The cutting of firewood is prohibited year-round.

(i) For more information on camping restrictions and specific hunting season dates, visit the Texas Parks & Wildlife website or call the Sam Houston National Forest district office (see Appendix F for details).

When choosing a primitive campsite, consider the following factors:

Impact on nature – Try to camp in previously used sites or areas clear of vegetation and out of sight of the trail. If you have to set up a new spot, make sure it is at least 200 feet away from trails and water sources. Always keep a clean camp and store food securely away from easy access by animals. Human waste should be buried at least 12 inches deep and 200 feet away from campsites, trails, and water sources. Pack out used toilet paper in zip lock bags to minimize the impact on nature.

Safety – Do not camp under or around dead trees! Falling trees and limbs (so-called "widow-makers") are a known safety hazard in Sam Houston National Forest and should not be underestimated, especially during windy conditions. Make sure to always check overhead first before choosing a campsite in the woods.

Comfort – Look for surfaces composed of dry sand or small gravel rather than organic substances and vegetation. This will prevent moisture from creeping into your tent from underneath. Similarly, moisture and dew collect faster the closer you are to water. Stay clear of wet areas in order to avoid soaked gear or even a solid layer of ice on your tent overnight. Additionally, this may also spare you some trouble with mosquitoes.

Hiker Camps

Hiker camps are designated primitive campsites along the trail, identified by metal markers painted with a blue tent symbol. Hikers can expect to find cleared areas with even surfaces. A few camps even provide tent pads and fire rings. However, no facilities, potable water sources, or other luxuries are available at any of them. Hiker camps are walk-in only, no reservations are required or fees charged.

Hunter Camps

Hunter camps are car-accessible, open fields or roads in the woods. Some of them are equipped with information boards that display important hunting and hiking information. Hunter camps don't provide numbered campsites, facilities, potable water sources, or other amenities. They are walk-in only, no reservations required or fees charged.

Developed Campgrounds

There are five developed campgrounds located adjacent to or in close proximity of the LSHT: Kelly's Pond (mile 14.3+1.2), Cagle (mile 16.0+2.7), Stubblefield (mile 19.7), Huntsville State Park (mile 35.7+2.2), and Double Lake (mile 75.0). They each have their individual amenities and incur different fees. Since prior reservation may be required, campgrounds are further detailed as part of the long lead items in Section 4d *Trail Shelters*.

Table 7 provides a list of available camping options along the LSHT including mileages to facilitate individual itinerary planning.

Mile	Camping Option
5.1+0.6	Sand Branch Trail hiker camp
6.3	Wilderness hiker camp
6.8+1.2	Pole Creek Trail hiker camp
11.8+0.5	Caney Creek hiker camp
14.3	Kelly's Pond Road hunter camp
14.3+1.2	Kelly's Pond Campground
16.0+2.7	Cagle Campground
19.7	Stubblefield Campground
20.3	Stubblefield overflow hunter camp
28.8	West Huntsville hiker camp
35.7+2.2	Huntsville State Park Campground
38.3	Phelps hiker camp
45.0	Four Notch hunter camp
51.3	East Four Notch hiker camp
59.8	Big Woods hiker camp

68.6	LSHT hiker camp #2 (tent pad + fire ring)
75.0	Double Lake Campground
75.6	LSHT hiker camp #1
83.5+0.6	Tarkington hunter camp
83.6	Tarkington hiker camp
88.9	Mercy hiker camp

Table 7 – Camping Options

e. Water

Water is available along the LSHT with quantities and qualities varying greatly depending on weather conditions. The most reliable resupply options are campgrounds and public water taps, which usually provide potable water year-round. A number of ponds, rivers, and permanent creeks along the trail provide water of decent quality even during severe droughts. The majority of small creeks and streams winding through the Sam Houston National Forest are seasonal. They will only carry decent quality water during very wet conditions and usually dry up during hot conditions. Droughts can occur at any time of year.

It is advisable to depend primarily on reliable water sources when planning a thru-hike on the LSHT, especially during periods when hot conditions or extreme heat are likely to occur. Having seasonal creeks and ponds as optional water sources along the trail is certainly beneficial, but making them a vital part of your resupply strategy is not recommended. After all, carrying a few extra pounds of water is much more bearable and less critical than running out because an expected water source is dry.

 As a rule of thumb, the average hiker will consume approx. one gallon of water per day, including meal preparation.

Always filter and treat any water coming from natural sources prior to consumption. Even though the water may look clear, it could potentially be contaminated with waterborne parasites or bacteria. Protozoan Giardia lamblia and the E.coli bacteria are prevalent globally. When exposed to, they cause diarrhea and abdominal cramps, sometimes even with a delay of 5-15 days. Fortunately, both can be filtered out and/or killed with common treatment methods, which are discussed further in Section 6d *Food & Water*.

! In order to avoid contamination of natural water sources, keep at least a distance of 100 feet when washing yourself, your clothing, or cooking utensils. Use bio-degradable soap or, ideally, refrain from using any kind of detergent altogether. Furthermore, leftover food and human waste should be buried at least 12 inches deep and 200 feet away from water sources.

Table 8 provides a selection of natural and potable water sources most likely to carry water year-round. Their corresponding LSHT mileages have been included as well to facilitate individual itinerary planning.

! Water from Camelia Lake near mile 32.0 should be avoided due to contamination with fertilizer and pesticides.

Mile	Water Source
2.55	Pond on right
3.95	Low volume spring-fed creek
9.76	Pond 150 yards to the left (north)
16.0+2.7	Cagle Campground (potable water)
16.5	Lake Conroe
17.9	Semi-permanent creek
19.7	Stubblefield Campground (potable water)
24.0	Small intermittent creek (Fern Creek)
32.0	Potable water tap on outside of City of Huntsville Pump House (small brick building)
33.2	Shallow spring-fed permanent creek (Alligator Creek)
35.7+2.2	Huntsville State Park Campground (potable water)
48.2	Boswell Creek
51.5	Pond on left
58.5	Off-trail pond indicated by new signage

65.0	Potable water tap on outside of Evergreen Baptist Church (church has given hikers permission to use tap behind the sanctuary)
71.1	San Jacinto River East Fork
72.2	Small intermittent stream
75.0	Double Lake Campground (potable water)
79.7	Final crossing of Big Creek
85.0	Pond 150 feet on left (east) (dam visible from trail)
86.8	Small pond on left (east)
92.5	San Jacinto River East Fork
95.8	Winters Bayou (river)

Table 8 – Water Sources

! The above listed water sources appeared to be dependable at the time of writing. However, conditions can change unexpectedly and a sufficient supply of water is crucial. Therefore, always confirm actual conditions and water availability prior to venturing onto the LSHT.

f. Safety

In order to have the safest possible experience, consider the following safety tips and potential hazards.

Heat Exhaustion

Heat exhaustion is caused by excessive exposure to high temperatures that is often accompanied by dehydration. Thru-hiking the LSHT bears an increased risk due to the hot and humid East Texas climate. Hikers are advised to thoroughly acquaint themselves with symptoms of and proper treatment for heat exhaustion.

River Crossings

During heavy rain, creeks and rivers can rise out of their banks quickly and unexpectedly, making a safe passage more difficult or even impossible. The most popular example is the San Jacinto River East Fork crossing. Refrain from fording rivers, creeks, and streams unless you are 100% certain that water levels and flow speeds warrant a safe passage. Exercise caution when using bridges and boardwalks as their structure may have been weakened or damaged during previous flooding.

Dead Trees

Dead trees or limbs, so-called "widow makers", are a natural part of the Sam Houston National Forest. They can be hazardous, especially during high winds, sometimes even prompting the closure of entire areas within the forest. Warning signs posted at trailheads indicate particularly dangerous sections. If wind conditions worsen, try to leave the woods or seek open spaces. Large fallen tree trunks can offer some protection if you are stuck in the forest.

Hunting

Hunting is allowed throughout the Sam Houston National Forest usually from late September through early January, except within the protected Big Creek Scenic Area where it is prohibited entirely. Hikers need to be aware of the different hunting seasons and make sure to wear highly visible colors during those time periods. Bright orange vests are a common recommendation.

Plants

The Sam Houston National Forest is home to a large variety of plant species of which some have the potential to be harmful to humans. Poison oak and poison ivy are probably the biggest concern as they are known to cause itching and allergic skin rashes when touched. These woody vines or shrubs have solid green leaves that hang from the stem in groups of three. Leaves can change color with the seasons (from solid greed in spring, to yellow and red in fall). Hikers may also see different species of fruits, berries, and mushrooms along the trail. In general, it is advisable to refrain from touching or consuming any of those unless you are 100% certain it is safe to do so.

Reptiles

There are four venomous types of snakes in East Texas that hikers need to be aware of: Coral Snake, Copperhead, Cottonmouth (Water Moccasin) and Rattlesnake. While encounters are rather rare, it is a good idea to educate yourself about these snakes and how to avoid them as best as possible. In addition, be aware that American alligators are infrequently spotted near large water reservoirs within the Sam Houston National Forest.

Insects

Flies, mosquitoes, and ticks pose the most immediate threat to hikers' well-being on the LSHT. They are not only particularly bothersome, but could potentially carry diseases, such as Lyme disease, and cause illness. Insects are present and active in Sam Houston National Forest year-round with numbers drastically increasing during the humid summer months. Always carry insect repellent, wear long sleeve shirts and pants, and check for ticks regularly.

Spiders

Texas has two venomous species of spiders, the black widow and the brown recluse. They are commonly found in undisturbed outdoor and indoor areas, e.g., woodpiles, bushes, toilets. Neither species is aggressive but will bite when accidentally trapped, disturbed, or threatened. Most spiders encountered along the trail are not venomous, however, hikers should educate themselves about the venomous species and how to best avoid them.

Prescribed Burns

Prescribed burns are controlled fires within administrative subunits (compartments) of the Sam Houston National Forest. They are conducted by forest authorities to safely reduce excessive amounts of forest fuels (brush, shrubs, and trees) in order to minimize damages in the event of wildfires. Be sure to check the U. S. Forest Service website for current burn notifications and most recent information prior to venturing onto the trail. The website also provides a map of compartments scheduled to be burnt within a given year, which may be useful information for itinerary planning purposes.

Road Walking

There are a few sections of the LSHT where you will be required to cross or walk along busy roads and even highways. Unless you decide to spare your legs a few asphalt miles by hitchhiking, walk as far on the shoulder as possible and pay particular attention to approaching trucks and agricultural machinery. Those vehicles can be quite massive, and their drivers may not be able to notice you in time, if at all.

Private Properties

When passing by private properties or small communities along the trail, watch out for dogs that roam around freely. They are usually just curious and will escort you for a bit, but should definitely be left alone. Do not enter or trespass private land. Not only because respecting people's privacy and property will help maintain the friendly relationship between hikers and residents, but also because you would not want to be mistaken for an intruder in an area where the possession of hunting weapons is common.

General Precautions

Whether you are hiking solo or with a buddy, it is always a good idea to inform a third party about your detailed hiking plans. In addition, you will find boxes with sign-in sheets at each of the LSHT trailheads. It is recommended to enter your information there as it will enable authorities to determine your location faster in case of emergency. Be aware that cell phone reception is not reliable in Sam Houston National Forest. Carrying a simple whistle will increase your chances of getting help sooner in case of emergency. Some hikers may even opt to bring a satellite-based handheld device along.

g. Flora & Fauna

The Sam Houston National Forest is home to a large number of wildlife species and abundant vegetation. Below is a brief overview of particularly prominent plants and animals, as well as potential hazards associated with them.

Vegetation

The Sam Houston National Forest is part of a larger ecological region called Piney Woods, which spans most of East Texas, harboring a large variety of tree and plant species. Historically, longleaf pines were dominating the top of the ridges in the national forest. Wildfires helped maintain these long and narrow trees along with the open savanna habitat surrounding them. However, over-harvesting of longleaf pines for more than a century and the suppression of wildfires caused its population to decrease drastically.

Nowadays, loblolly pine, interspersed with shortleaf pine, dominate the Piney Woods. These fast growing species have a light seed that is easily transported by the wind. Their current predominance is further reinforced by fewer occurrences of natural wildfires, which historically kept their population confined. Loblolly pines can reach respectable heights of over 150 feet with 5 feet in diameter and a lifespan of 250+ years. As a result of ongoing commercial forestry, however, most of the existing pine population in the Sam Houston National Forest only reaches half that size.

Further down the ridge, oak and other hardwood species flourish in river bottoms and along creek channels. Trees, usually more common in eastern areas, such as White oak and southern Magnolia, add to the transregional diversity. As do plants originating from drier western climates, such as prickly pear cacti and yucca.

The moist woodlands of the Sam Houston National Forest are home to a rich variety of mosses, grasses, ferns, and mushrooms. Groves of dwarf palmetto grow thick in the extensive swamps of the national forest which also create a habitat for unique species, such as carnivorous pitcher plants, wild orchids, and sundews. The large diversity of wildflowers and flowering shrubs creates a magnificent blaze of colors during blossom, which is a spectacle worthwhile experiencing.

(i) A great way to learn more about the plant life of the national forest while being out in nature is to join one of the expert-led group outings organized by the LSHT Club.

Wildlife

The immense biodiversity of the Piney Woods region is also reflected in animal life. Hikers walking the LSHT will likely see white-tailed deer grazing in the evenings and feral hogs[4] digging up forest soil in search of roots and small insects in the mornings. The nine-banded armadillo has migrated north from Mexico and is now commonly seen along the trail. The largest predators in East Texas are coyotes and bobcats. There are even reports of roaming mountain lions and black bears, but sightings remain extremely rare.

River otters have recovered from brink of extinction and are now more frequently spotted by patient observers. Other mammal species more commonly found in East Texas include raccoon, eastern fox squirrel, gray squirrel and opossum. Invasive species such as the nutria, a large, semi-aquatic exotic rodent, are also common but rather unpopular because of their detrimental impact on the native ecosystem.

Texas is often cited as being a bird watching paradise. The rich habitats support a diversity of resident and migratory species. Hikers can listen to the beautiful songs of the brown-headed nuthatch, wood thrush, and different types of new world warbler. Additional ambient sounds are created by pileated and red-headed woodpeckers, usually pecking away in the bottomlands of the forest. The rare red-cockaded woodpecker prefers open pine habitats with large trees and is often spotted near Stubblefield

---

[4] Wild hogs originating from domestic breeds that either escaped or were released for hunting purposes. With each generation, the hog's domestic characteristics diminished and they developed the traits needed for survival in the wild.

Lake and Huntsville State Park. Look overhead for black vulture, turkey vulture, red-shouldered hawk, red-tailed hawk, and common nighthawk.

During winter, the warm East Texas climate attracts another endangered species that has returned from brink of extinction, the bald eagle. Frequent sightings occur near larger water reservoirs like Lake Conroe and Stubblefield Lake, and even along the San Jacinto River. Lakes and river banks are also excellent areas to watch for feeding herons and egrets. Other birds to look out for include eastern kingbird, summer tanager, eastern phoebe, and indigo bunting.

East Texas is also home to a large variety of amphibians and reptiles. Many types of frogs, toads, and salamanders, e.g., the marbled salamander, inhabit the wetlands. Lizards, such as the green anole, prefer the drier areas of the forest. The same goes for the many species of snakes, of which most are harmless, such as the eastern hognose snake. The few venomous types have already been discussed in Section 3f *Safety*.

The grass- and bottomlands of the national forest provide a rich habitat for box turtles and the Texas tortoise. The American alligator, another species that has yet to recover from near extinction, is the largest reptile found in Sam Houston National Forest. They may occasionally be spotted basking in the sun along the shores of large water reservoirs, such as Lake Raven in Huntsville State Park.

The Piney Woods are also inhabited by an amazing variety of insects. While flies, mosquitoes, and ticks are rather bothersome, the numerous species of butterflies and dragonflies are much more pleasant hiking companions. Butterflies commonly seen along the trail include giant and tiger swallowtail, silvery checkerspot, red admiral, and monarch. Dragonflies, such as great blue skimmer, cobra clubtail, eastern ringtail, and regal darner, can be observed darting among bank vegetation or scattered about pond areas.

4. Long Lead Items

Planning a thru-hike on a popular long-distance trail, such as the LSHT, usually includes items that require more lead time than others. This chapter introduces items that are generally more time-sensitive from a budget as well as general availability perspective and should therefore be addressed early on in the planning process.

a. Permits & Regulations

For the most part, the rules that govern hikers on the LSHT are the same as those that govern any person in the surrounding Sam Houston National Forest. The big exception is that motorized vehicles, bicycles, and horses are prohibited on the LSHT. Only foot travel is allowed. Hiking on the trail, primitive overnight camping along the trail, and parking in LSHT trailhead parking lots does not require a permit. However, parking or camping in nearby developed campgrounds or state parks will usually incur a fee. Dogs are permitted on the LSHT, but must be leashed and under the owner's control at all times.

Hunting is allowed in Sam Houston National Forest and on adjacent private properties usually from late September through early January, except within the protected Big Creek Scenic Area where it is prohibited entirely. This is important to be aware of not only for safety reasons, but also for planning purposes since camping is restricted to developed campgrounds, hiker camps, and hunter camps during those times. Recreational fishing in public waters of Texas requires a fishing license with the appropriate stamp endorsement. Licenses are not required if fishing within a state park or on Free Fishing Day, held each year on the first Saturday in June.

!	Sections of the LSHT follow along private properties or pass directly through them. In those areas, hikers are advised to pay particular attention to signs and to respect people's privacy. It is everyone's responsibility to ensure property owners will continue to allow foot passage across their land.

b. Hiking Buddy

The decision to thru-hike the LSHT or any other long-distance trail by oneself, with a hiking partner, or even as a group may be driven by practical considerations, financial implications, safety concerns, or simply personal preference. Especially, if this is your first multi-day hike, a friend by your side can help navigate through unfamiliar terrain, deal with unexpected obstacles, or keep spirits up as energy levels fade.

Finding the right companion can be a challenging endeavor in itself and should be given thorough thought. The following questions may aid you in your decision-making process when looking for potential candidates:

- Will you be comfortable being around that person 24/7 for the entire duration of your trip?
- Do all of you have somewhat similar fitness levels and hiking experience?
- Do all of you share similar interests and expectations (e.g., taking lots of photos, off-trail relaxing/exploring)?

If you decide to look for a hiking partner, approach people early so they have sufficient time to carefully assess if they are capable of the challenge and whether or not they have the necessary resources at their disposal. Potential doubts and concerns should be discussed openly and sorted out well before hitting the trail.

With regard to gear and supplies, traveling alone or with others can make a difference, but not necessarily a big one. Usually, you can share a stove, pot, water purifier, first aid kit, pocket knife, emergency rope, map, shovel, and a camera. These items can add up to approximately 4lbs. Sharing that weight with one person would save each of you 2lbs and in a group of four, the individual pack weight would be reduced by 3lbs. Sharing other gear items may be more difficult or simply undesirable. Sharing a tent, for example, could potentially save additional weight. However, being able to retreat into your own shelter after a long day of hiking may be well worth carrying a few extra pounds.

In case of emergency, it is obviously good to have someone close-by. Solo hikers may find themselves walking long stretches of the LSHT without meeting another person, especially during the week when the trail is usually less heavily frequented. Hikers venturing off on their own are advised to take additional precautions to make sure help will arrive within reasonable time in case of emergency.

For various reasons, it may not always be possible to find a hiking buddy for a particular trip. You may also just make the conscious decision to venture off on your own to test your physical abilities and mental strength while experiencing absolute solitude. Hiking the LSHT alone is a viable option and quite common. Carrying the necessary gear and supplies by yourself is absolutely manageable.

c. Travel Arrangements

Even though the LSHT is not too far from civilization, getting to and from the main trailheads takes some planning. Depending on where you are coming from and which direction you plan to walk the LSHT, there are different options to consider. Figure 6 provides an overview of major towns and traffic routes near the trail as well as airport connections and car rental locations.

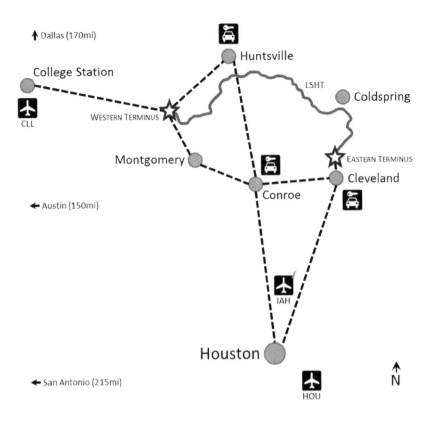

Figure 6 – Overview of Travel Options

Traveling by Car

Driving a car to the LSHT is probably the most flexible option. All trailheads are easily accessible, parking is free, and there are no restrictions on what you can pack. Obviously, this option may only be viable for people living within driving distance of the trail. If you decide to travel by car and plan to park it at one of the two termini, keep the following things in mind:

Firstly, you will need one-way transportation to either get to the start or back from the finish. Unless you have someone who can pick you up, your options may be limited to hitchhiking or taking a taxi. If you decide to go with the latter option, it is advisable to make the necessary arrangements in advance as cell phone service is rather unreliable throughout Sam Houston National Forest. For details refer to section 'Taxi Service' below.

Secondly, there is no surveillance at any of the trailhead parking lots. The number of reported theft or vandalism incidents is relatively small, however, it is always advisable not to leave any valuables in your car or, at least, to store them out of sight, e.g., in the trunk.

(i) Park your car at the final trailhead and catch a ride to the start. This approach may save you additional hassle after a long and exhausting hike. Also, leaving extra food, water, clothes, and perhaps a little celebratory treat in your car may add to the excitement when crossing the finish line.

Traveling by Airplane

Three airports provide access to the LSHT if driving is not an option: George Bush Intercontinental Airport (IAH), William P. Hobby Airport (HOU), and Easterwood Airport (CLL). All three are serviced by major airlines and car rentals. Table 9 provides an overview of available car rentals and their respective pick-up and drop-off locations near Sam Houston National Forest.

Location	Avis	Budget	Enterprise	Hertz
Cleveland	-	-	x	x
Conroe	x	x	x	x
Huntsville	-	-	x	x

Table 9 – Car Rentals near Sam Houston National Forest

None of the car rental offices is located in close vicinity to the main trailheads. Thus, you will need to either arrange for additional transportation or hitchhike the last stretch. Some of the car rentals offer a pick-up service which could potentially help you get from the Eastern Terminus to Cleveland or vice versa. Make sure to reserve your car in advance and to check individual office hours, especially when planning on picking up your car on a weekend.

! When traveling by airplane, be aware that there are restrictions on what is allowed in your carry-on and checked luggage. For example, any kind of fuel is generally prohibited, which includes camping stove cartridges. Make sure to familiarize yourself with those restrictions and plan to pick up prohibited items at local stores prior to venturing onto the trail.

Taxi Service

Whether you decide to drive your own car or plan to arrive by airplane, chances are you will require additional transportation at some point or simply to get from one end of the trail to the other. Unfortunately, public transportation is not a viable option, so you are left with either hitchhiking or taking a cab. The latter will cost you approximately $2.25 per mile.

It is highly recommended to make arrangements in advance as there are only a few taxi companies that offer to drive passengers all the way to the trailheads. Below are two examples of companies that have been reliable in the past, but hikers are encouraged to shop around and inquire about individual services and pricing.

- Taxi 24 LLC: 702 Cartwright Rd, Conroe, TX 77301, Phone: 1 (936) 756-8294
- City Cab Taxi: 916 Mccall Ave, Conroe, TX 77301, Phone: 1 (936) 539-4455

i Have driving directions handy as not all cab drivers are familiar with the LSHT and cell phone reception is limited throughout Sam Houston National Forest. It is also advisable to bring enough money in cash as many payment options that require a data connection may not work.

d. Trail Shelters

In addition to the many primitive camping options along the LSHT, hikers may opt to take advantage of the five campgrounds, which are located adjacent to or in close proximity of the trail, and their respective amenities.

Criteria	Kelly's Pond	Cagle	Stubblefield	Huntsville SP	Double Lake
LSHT mile	14.3+1.2	16.0+2.7	19.7	35.7+2.2	75.0
Tent campsites	8	45	28	60	12
Features	Picnic tables, fire rings, lantern posts	Tent pads, picnic tables, fire rings	Tent pads, picnic tables, fire rings	Picnic tables, fire rings, lantern posts	Tent pads, picnic tables, fire rings
Daily rate	Free	$27	$15	$15 (+ $5 daily entrance fee)	$18
Reservation	First-come, first-served only (overflow camp nearby)	Online/phone reservations; FCFS for un-reserved sites	First-come, first-served only (overflow camp nearby)	Online/phone reservations; FCFS for un-reserved sites	Online/phone reservations; FCFS for un-reserved sites
Potable water	No	Yes	Yes	Yes	Yes
Restrooms	Vault toilets only	Flush toilets, sinks, warm showers	Flush toilets, sinks, warm showers	Flush toilets, sinks, warm showers	Flush toilets, sinks, warm showers
Food	No	No	No	Snacks, vending machine	Snacks, vending machine
Electricity	No	Yes	Yes	Yes	Yes
Contact info	Forest Service (USDA) 1-936-344-6205			Huntsville SP 1-936-295-5644	Double Lake RA 1-936-653-3448

Table 10 – Trail Shelters

All campgrounds require visitors to bring their own shelter, e.g., tent or hammock, and reservations may have to be made in advance. Table 10 above provides specifics on available campground options, their individual amenities, costs, and reservation policies.

(i) There is a central website for campground reservations, closures, and general information (*http://www.recreation.gov*). The website does not include Huntsville State Park, which has its own website (*http://tpwd.texas.gov/state-parks/huntsville*).

Figure 7 – Huntsville State Park and Double Lake Recreation Area Campsites

If a particular circumstance forces you to leave the forest for a night, or if you simply choose to, suitable accommodation options may be available in the neighboring towns shown in Figure 6 on page 36, with Coldspring and Huntsville being the closest ones. Below are two options that require only a relatively short side trip from the LSHT.

- San Jacinto Inn in Coldspring
  Distance: ca. 2.5mi from Double Lake Rec. Area (mile 75.0)
  Address: 13815 Anthony Ln, Coldspring, TX 77331
  Phone: 1 (936) 653-3008
- Oakview Manor Bed & Breakfast in Huntsville
  Distance: ca. 2.8 miles from LSHT path (mile 35.0)
  Address: 7137 St Hwy 75 N, Huntsville, TX 77340
  Phone: 1 (936) 295-3352
  Web: http://www.oakviewmanorbnb.com

5. Planning & Preparation

While the remoteness of the LSHT allows for exceptional biodiversity, it also calls for proper advance preparation. The planning effort is manageable and absolutely worth it. Using the detailed information and guidance provided in this chapter will help you carefully and effectively prepare your trip, which will make your experience all the more enjoyable and rewarding.

a. Itinerary

Planning the itinerary is a two-step process. The first step includes all activities concerning long lead items. The resulting 'macro-plan' is the organizational frame of the hiking trip. The second step focuses on determining the specifics of your thru-hike. The resulting 'micro-plan' is your personal hiking strategy.

Macro-Planning

The below flow chart outlines the important steps in planning your overall trip. The order shown was determined based on pragmatic considerations but may be altered depending on personal preferences. Individual steps may also be omitted if not applicable.

Figure 8 – Flow Chart Macro Planning

The first four steps address the general timing of your trip. Estimating your days on the trail will give you a good idea of the duration of the trip. Based on the duration, you can then check your schedule and determine potential travel dates. During this step, it is advisable to incorporate seasonal weather-related aspects as discussed in Section 3c *Weather*. Once you have determined your preliminary dates, make sure to check the hunting calendar as well as the controlled burn schedule. Both activities may pose additional restrictions on your hiking schedule. However, dates are available far in advance, so incorporating this information in your macro-plan shouldn't be too difficult.

Once you have determined your preliminary schedule, you can then use it to find a hiking partner, unless you plan to hike solo. It is usually easier to convince people to join if you have a more concrete plan to present. Plus, it's usually easier to discuss options that have already been narrowed down compared to options that are wide open. Once you have confirmed your dates in general and with your potential hiking buddy, you can start thinking about travel arrangements. Especially, when you are traveling from out-of-state or even outside the country, getting started on flights, accommodation, car rental, and other bookings early on will increase your chances of getting the preferred options and better deals overall.

If you plan to stay at one of the developed campgrounds along trail, it may be advisable to reserve the required number of spots in advance. However, in order to being able to do so, you will have to have a better idea of your actual hiking itinerary. Therefore, reserving spots at developed campgrounds is a macro-planning step that partially overlaps with micro-planning activities.

Micro-Planning

The goal of this planning step is to map out your personal hiking strategy. The first task is to confirm your initial ETD from Section 2b *Time*. Based on your final ETD, you will be able to derive your average daily mileage which constitutes the foundation of your hiking itinerary. Make sure to include the extra time and mileage for any side trips you are planning to do. If you plan to do any zero days, make sure to incorporate those in your itinerary as well. However, zero days will not impact your average daily mileage.

For example, let's assume the final ETD is 9, including one zero day, but no side trips or off-the-trail resupply trips. This translates to 12 miles per day on average, taking into consideration that zero days don't count towards the calculation:

$$96 \text{ miles} / (9\text{-}1) \text{ days} = 12 \text{ miles/day}$$

The 12 miles/day estimate serves as the basis for determining the actual distances targeted for each individual day. Actual daily distances may need to be adjusted based on available water sources, difficulty of the trail section, and preferred camping options. If you consider resupplying food at some point during your trip, the required stops or detours should be incorporated as well.

Using the compact trail guide in Appendix B in combination with the average mile estimate will help you further delineate your daily distances. To continue our example, we are taking the 12 miles and start looking for potential campsites for day 1. Caney Creek hiker camp at mile 11.8+0.5 seems to be a good fit. Analyzing the first 12 miles further, we realize that there are three water sources along the way, and no particularly challenging trail sections are to be expected. As a result, it is reasonable to assume the target of 12 miles for the first day will be achieved and you can mark your compact trail guide accordingly (as indicated in Table 11).

Mile	Trail Feature
0.0	TH#1; Western Terminus; start of Wilderness Section (8.7 miles)
2.55	**Pond on right**
3.5	TH#2
3.95	**Low volume spring-fed creek**
5.1+0.6	Sand Branch Trail hiker camp
6.3	Wilderness hiker camp
6.8+1.2	Pole Creek Trail hiker camp
8.7	TH#3; start of Kelly Section (7.3 miles)
9.76	**Pond 150 yards to the left (north)**
11.8+0.5	**Caney Creek hiker camp** **[DAY 1]**
14.3	Kelly's Pond Road hunter camp
14.3+1.2	Kelly's Pond Campground
16.0	TH#6; start of Stubblefield Section (12.8 mi)

16.0+2.7	Cagle Recreation Area
16.5	**Great view of Lake Conroe**
17.9	**Semi-permanent creek**
19.7	**Stubblefield Lake Recreation Area** **[DAY 2a]**
20.3	Stubblefield overflow hunter camp; trail enters woods to the right (across from overflow camp), after 300ft the trail takes a sharp left (watch as there is a trail that goes straight!)
23.5	Sharp left onto road FS 243, then right into woods after 150 feet
24.0	**Small intermittent creek (Fern Creek)**
24.5	Turn right onto road FS 243, follow for 0.2 miles, trail turns left at hikers sign
26.4	Turn right onto unmarked gravel road (Bath Ln), follow for 1.5 miles, turn right onto paved road (Ball Rd), follow for 0.15 miles, turn left onto gravel Cotton Creek Cemetery Road (past cattle guard), follow for 0.5 miles, take right fork onto unmarked road FS 287 (past auto gate), trail enters woods on the right after 0.15 miles
28.8	**Start of Huntsville Section (6.2 miles); West Huntsville West Huntsville hiker camp** **[DAY 2b]**
31.1	Highest elevation (400 feet)
...	...

Table 11 – Itinerary Planning Example

Adding additional 12 miles for day 2 will get you to approx. mile 24 which is right in between Stubblefield Campground (mile 19.7) and West Huntsville hiker camp (mile 28.8). Now, you could decide to aim for one of these campsite, consequently either subtracting or adding approx. 4 miles, or simply setup a primitive camp at mile 24 to stick to the original mileage goal.

> [!] Be careful when attempting to exceed your daily average miles by more than 20% and make sure to have a fallback option in case your ambitious plan does not work out.

Repeat this process for each day of your trip. Use caution when planning side trips and be sure to factor them in correctly as they are not included in the compact trail guide by default. Also, make sure to properly account for the following two crucial facets of the trail: Camping is prohibited within the protected Big Creek Scenic Area (miles 78.6-80.8), and you may be forced to take the 3-mile unmarked unofficial detour around the East Fork of the San Jacinto River (mile 71.1) if crossing is unsafe or even impossible due to high water levels.

(i) Even under normal conditions, chances are you will get at least your feet wet when fording the San Jacinto River. It may be worth thinking about what time of the day will be best for doing so. The same applies to crossing the spillway near Camelia Lake (mile 32.0).

(!) Keep a close watch on the weather forecast and check in with the U. S. Forest Service regarding the water level at the San Jacinto River East Fork prior to venturing onto the trail. If necessary, make last minute adjustments to your itinerary in order to prepare for possible unfavorable conditions. Undoubtedly, you would not want to get to the East Fork crossing without having thought about a backup plan and then realize it is impossible to ford.

For additional help with planning your personal itinerary, have a look at the examples provided in Appendix D. There, you will find three itinerary suggestions based on different walking speeds – fast, moderate, and relaxed.

b. Training

For many readers, thru-hiking the LSHT will be their greatest challenge to date, physically and mentally. Don't be afraid to accept it! Proper training will significantly increase your chance of success, improve the quality of your days on the trail, and decrease the chance of overuse injuries. Ultimately, with the right level of fitness and a positive mindset, you will revel in your accomplishment and soon seek the next one.

Mental Preparation

The right attitude, in every phase of a long-distance hike, is just as important as proper physical and logistical preparation. From the moment you make the decision, through the weeks of planning your trip, to the final day on the trail, maintaining an open mind and a resilient attitude in coping with obstacles is essential. At any given point, you may be confronted with fatigue, anxiety, or doubt. In those moments, remind yourself that even the smallest steps in the right direction will help you achieve the goal eventually.

Physical Preparation

Endurance and strength are indispensable assets when it comes to going the full distance of a thru-hike. If your body is not used to walking long distances on a daily basis while carrying the extra weight of up to 40lbs, it will need proper conditioning. Individual workout needs may vary based on age, health, current fitness level, and other factors. However, the general intention is to get your body moving and comfortable with being active early on, and then gradually increase the intensity.

A good training routine will incorporate cardiovascular exercises and weight lifting elements. Go hiking frequently and participate in other forms of aerobic fitness like cycling, swimming, running, or group fitness classes. This will not only increase your endurance, but also build confidence and momentum for your adventure. In addition, it is advisable to exercise with light to medium weights to strengthen shoulder and back muscles.

A good exercise example is the "90-degree dumbbell lateral raise". Stand with your feet at shoulder's width, your back slightly slanted forward, and your core muscles engaged. Start by holding the weights in your hands with your elbows at a 90-degree angle touching your ribs and your forearms extended straight in front of your body. In a slow, smooth motion, raise elbows from your ribs to shoulder's height. Hold briefly and return into the starting position.

(i) Choose a weight that allows you to do at least three sets of 15-20 repetitions and remember to engage both your abdominal as well as your lower back muscles to support a sturdy stance.

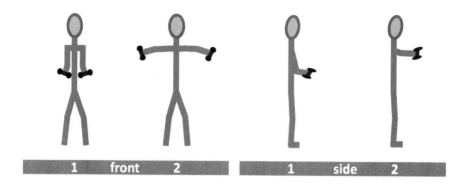

Figure 9 – 90 Degree Dumbbell Lateral Raise

As your fitness level develops, it is crucial to add weight to some of your cardio exercises to simulate the backpack you will be carrying on the trail. Begin wearing an empty pack, then a partially weighted pack, and eventually the equivalent weight of what you plan to carry during the trip. For an even better training effect, you could gradually progress your practice hikes to steeper terrain. However, given the rather flat profile of the LSHT, such level of preparation is not necessarily required.

Hiking Style

It is helpful to adopt a good hiking style in order for you to use your energy efficiently and to keep strains to your joints and tendons to a minimum. This includes hiking at a sustainable pace and taking small controlled steps.

The LSHT is an ultra-marathon, not a sprint. From an athletic perspective, this means that you need to keep your metabolism and energy conversion in an aerobic state. In brief, aerobic metabolism means that your muscles are receiving enough oxygen from your lungs, sufficient fuel through your bloodstream, and have enough time to dispose of by-products from burning the fuel, especially lactic acid.

The aerobic state or respiration is usually the sweet spot for your body to process its energy, from a nutritional intake as well as fat storage perspective. Keep in mind that even very fit people have an average body fat level of 5-15 percent. That means that a 160lbs person would have around 16lbs of fat which contain approx. 56,000 calories – enough caloric energy for over 20 days. This body fat is a valuable reserve you should tap on the trail in order to keep your packed food weight low and potentially reduce your body weight as a pleasant side effect. Maintaining a sustainable pace allows you to do just that.

Finding your personal sustainable pace is simple. It is the pace at which you breathe deeply, but not rushed, you may sweat, but never excessively, you feel you could hike this way for hours without having to stop for extended breaks frequently. As a result, a slow but sustainable pace will be the fastest way, because you will feel less fatigue and need less rest/recovery time.

In addition to maintaining a sustainable pace, it is advisable to focus on taking small controlled steps. Doing so will avoid stress peaks for your muscles and reduce the force of impact on your joints. Scrambling down and up deep river beds with a full backpack can be particularly hard on knees and ankles. The larger the step, the greater the vertical drop and, hence, the impact on you joints.

Small steps are also less likely to go wrong. The LSHT has varying trail conditions. You will walk on uneven ground, loose gravel, muddy soil, and all kinds of wet and slippery surfaces. A small step has less momentum that could potentially cause you to twist your ankle or slip and, thus, will minimize the likelihood of a misstep injury.

Trekking Poles

Various forums and literature state that the proper use of trekking poles may increase your daily distance by up to 25%. Regardless of whether or not this is accurate for you, there are some definite advantages to hiking with poles that are a little easier to grasp.

More stability and balance – When carrying a heavy pack, especially one in which the weight is not evenly distributed, you can easily lose your balance. Having two extra points of contact with the trail, you are less likely to slip in the first place, and slips are less likely to turn into falls. On the LSHT, trekking poles will help maintain balance and increase stability when navigating over and around trail obstacles (e.g., stream and river crossings), traversing slippery logs and bog bridges, and wading through muddy terrain.

Less stress on joints and muscles – In addition to preventing falls, trekking poles reduce the impact of hiking on legs, knees, ankles, and feet. When going downhill, they can be used to slow down your forward movement, reducing the compressive force on your joints, in particular your knees. On steep ascents, poles help hikers maintain forward momentum by recruiting upper body muscles to the task, reducing the strain that would normally be absorbed by the lower body alone.

The propulsion aspect of the trekking poles is also important. Even though your legs will undoubtedly be doing most of the work, your upper body can support them. Walking with poles can help you establish and maintain a consistent rhythm, which can reduce overall fatigue and increase your speed. This is especially true on flatter, non-technical terrain.

| ! | When navigating steep terrain, it is important to find the right balance. Make sure not to overly strain your shoulders while trying to provide relieve to your legs.

When using hiking poles, make sure they are adjusted to the right length. This should be approx. 0.7 x your height. Securely lock your poles after adjusting. Then, when taking a stride with the left leg, set your right pole in front of your right, rear foot (Figure 10, step 3). In this position, smoothly but forcefully push back. Then, gently lift the right pole tip slightly above the ground as you bring the left pole forward. Place the left pole in front of your left, rear foot (Figure 10, step 5). Engage and repeat.

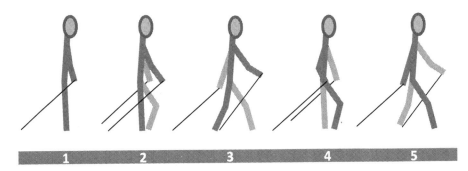

Figure 10 – Trekking Pole Use

Be sure not to ram the poles into the ground. This causes stress on your wrists and shoulders and leads to earlier exhaustion. Also, you don't want your energy to go straight into the ground, but rather into a forward movement. Note how in Figure 10 the poles are never vertical, but always at an angle so that you push forward and not down.

If you do decide to use trekking poles on the LSHT, make sure to familiarize yourself with the right technique. When used incorrectly, hiking poles can cause pain and injuries to shoulders and wrists. Also, allow yourself phases of rest from using your trekking poles. Hold them in their balanced-middle while hiking along flat, easy stretches of the trail, with your shoulders either dangling down loosely or keeping your natural walking stride motion without the poles touching the ground.

(i) Before taking poles on the LSHT, it is very helpful to try them out to see how they feel. Practice the motion which is a little different from your usual one. If you cannot get comfortable or find that poles cause additional exhaustion, leave it at that. Especially, if you already have problems with your shoulders or wrists, poles may cause unnecessary stress.

c. Food

When thru-hiking the LSHT, you will be dependent on your own food supply for the most part. There are no dining options immediately adjacent to the trail and only a few options to replenish snacks. However, having an adequate amount of food at your disposal is essential for reviving energy and keeping spirits up. Looking forward to a good meal is motivational and having a satisfied stomach lets you fall asleep more contentedly at night.

Putting effort into planning and preparing balanced meals with a lot of variety is well worth it. Refer to Appendix B for a comprehensive list of food suggestions. Nothing is worse than knowing you will have to eat something that is not the least bit enjoyable. Below are some guidelines to aid with choosing the right kind of food:

- Weight: your food should be as dry and light as possible (incl. packaging)
- Nutritional value: combine foods to ensure an adequate supply of vitamins and minerals
- Calorie distribution: balance approx. 15% protein, 60% carbohydrates, and 25% fat per meal
- Non-perishable: your food must not spoil for a week or longer in rather warm and humid conditions
- Easy preparation: save gas, time, dirty pots, and nerves after a long day of hiking

Two factors are particularly important to consider when determining how much food to bring – calorie value and space. Your meals should provide approx. 1.5-2 times the calories you usually consume per day. Calculate higher calories when in low temperatures and vice versa. Additional hunger can be satisfied with snacks. If you are planning to hike the LSHT without resupplying, you will have to be very conscious of what to bring, as everything must fit in your backpack along with the rest of the gear. Dealing with space restrictions usually outdoes weight issues. The less space you have, the less water and air content should be in your food packaging. This makes for a dense nutritional value.

 As a rule of thumb, you should aim for about 1-2lbs of food per person per day.

In order to avoid space issues, it helps to repackage your food into single servings, let out any air, and cut off excess packaging. Zip lock bags work well, they can be labeled and reused for packing out waste. If you choose to bring a sealable food canister, try to make layers of meals per day rather than locking in all breakfast items at the bottom, and so forth. This makes accessing your food more convenient. Furthermore, stack the most perishable food items at the top of your canister for early consumption.

In addition to your main meals, well-chosen snacks and supplements provide valuable nourishment as well. As temperatures rise, it is vital to replenish electrolytes, such as sodium, chloride, potassium, magnesium, manganese, and calcium, on a consistent basis. High water intake without electrolyte replacement over many hours can lead to hyponatremia, a life-threatening condition where your body does not have enough salts to function. Adding salty snacks (pretzels, goldfish, salted nuts, or chips) and/or supplements to your trail diet helps avoid electrolyte imbalance.

> ⚠ If you are on a low sodium diet, ask your doctor if a higher sodium intake on the trail would be appropriate for you.

As you plan your meals, mind the respective cooking times and utensils needed for preparation. Anything that requires boiling for over ten minutes can be bothersome. Similarly, in-camp preparations, such as cutting/peeling/mashing, or meals that require a lot of attention and flipping with spatulas can be a hassle after a long day of hiking. Many hikers plan their meals so that the only cooking gear required is a small gas stove, one pot, and one spoon. Nevertheless, whatever meals you decide to go with, bring along adequate equipment and know your own patience.

> ⚠ After preparing food at camp, do dishes at least 100 feet from your campsite. Also, be sure to pack any leftovers and store your food securely and at a safe distance away from camp to not attract any unwanted visitors.

Some hikers alternate their food strategy depending on the campsite, the arrival time, and the difficulty of the day ahead. Particularly nice areas and slow days may invite you to enjoy a nice morning coffee or spend a long evening with celebratory dining. In summary, your food strategy is a matter of personal preference, your hiking schedule, resupply strategy, and access to gas.

d. Resupply

People who plan to thru-hike the LSHT in less than a week may choose not to resupply during their trip. While it is certainly possible to carry enough food for such period of time, it is important to keep in mind that it will increase the overall pack weight. The average hiker will likely resupply at some point during their trip. Depending on the resupply strategy, this may require spending some time off the trail. Available options include caching supplies along the route, arranging for supplies to be dropped-off, sending a package to a pick-up location, and purchasing food and other goods at nearby stores.

Caching

Hikers who plan to arrive at the LSHT by car can choose to cache supplies along the route prior to venturing onto the trail. Convenient caching locations are trailheads, as they are easily accessible by car, and intersections of the trail with public roads. Please consider the following guidelines for dependable and responsible caching:

- Use only sturdy weather- and rodent-proof containers (five gallon plastic buckets from the hardware store with duct tape-sealed lids have proven to be practical)
- Clearly mark containers with ownership information and expected date of retrieval
- Stash containers in strategic locations (well-concealed and protected from the elements, if possible)
- Always retrieve cache containers after trip is completed (everything else is littering)
- Never move or take anything from caches you may accidentally come across (someone else's life may depend on those supplies)

Drop-Off

If you are fortunate enough to know someone who lives within reasonable distance of the Sam Houston National Forest, you may choose to arrange for supplies to be dropped off during your journey. Similar to caching, trailheads and intersections with public roads are probably the most convenient locations for this option.

Pick-up

Another strategy is to ship resupply packages to nearby post or park offices ahead of time, and then pick them up during your trip. United States Post Offices offer a service called "General Delivery" which allows you to ship packages to a designated office location, and they will hold it for up to 30 days. The USPS location closest to the LSHT is in Coldspring, TX. The detour for picking up your resupply would be approx. 5 miles round-trip from Double Lake Recreation Area. Should you decide to send yourself a package for general delivery, be sure to address it as follows:

[First & Last Name]
GENERAL DELIVERY
[Town], [State] [Zip Code]-9999
HOLD UNTIL: [Date]

(i) The zip code extension "-9999" indicates general delivery. For more information on specific post office locations and their business hours refer to *http://www.usps.com*.

The administration offices at Huntsville State Park and Double Lake Recreation Area may also be willing to receive and hold smaller packages for LSHT thru-hikers as a courtesy. It is recommended to coordinate the details with each location directly using the contact information provided in Section 4d *Trail Shelters*.

Similar to caching, choose a sturdy and watertight container when shipping your resupply to a pick-up location. The use of standard cardboard boxes is not recommended as they get easily damaged or wet, which could potentially compromise the shipped goods. Refrain from packing perishable goods and make sure not to include any restricted items, such as camping stove fuel, lighters, and other flammable substances. In addition to your planned meals and snacks for the trip, consider packing sweets and other goodies, toilet paper, batteries, sunscreen, vitamin & mineral supplements, blister treatment, bandages, and other small useful items.

Stores

Huntsville State Park and Double Lake Recreation Area have small convenience stores on-site, where visitors can purchase snack foods, beverages, and other everyday items. These stores are usually open on busy days and weekends, but may be closed when less visitors are to be expected. The limited range of goods and varying business hours practically rule out park stores as viable resupply options. Actual grocery stores can be found in the nearby towns of Huntsville and Coldspring. However, getting there from the LSHT and back can turn into a time- and energy-consuming endeavor.

6. Gear

The decision what gear to acquire and to carry with you on a particular trip generally depends on the hiking strategy, anticipated trail and weather conditions, personal preferences in terms of comfort and functionality, and ultimately the available budget. This chapter is intended as an overview of essential gear items and as a guide to support your LSHT-specific choices. Later on, you can compare your thoughts on gear with my personal experience and lessons learned in Chapter 7.

a. Clothing

When hiking, it is very important to choose proper clothing as you never want to be too hot or too cold. Picking the right clothing for the LSHT is particularly challenging as weather conditions can be very unpredictable at times. Below are some general tips on clothing along with LSHT-specific recommendations.

Avoid Cotton

When choosing the right clothing, there is one material you want to avoid at all cost – cotton! When you hike, you perspire, and any cotton clothing touching your skin will absorb moisture rather than wicking it away. Once saturated, cotton loses all its insulating properties and takes a long time to dry. Especially in very windy or cold conditions, this can lead to a dramatic drop in body temperature which should not be taken lightly.

Opt for fabrics that transport perspiration away from the skin quickly. Synthetics (polyester/polyester blends) and merino wool have excellent moisture-wicking capabilities. Synthetics dry faster than merino wool which is a big advantage during the hot and humid summer months in East Texas. Merino wool, however, allows for better temperature regulation and, thus, provides more comfort and warmth on cooler days. From a price perspective, synthetic fibers are definitely the more budget-friendly option compared to their natural counterparts.

Wear Layers

Layering your clothing will maximize your comfort on the trail. It is a simple, proven concept that allows you to make quick adjustments based on your activity level and changes in the weather. The latter of which is particularly relevant for hiking in East Texas. Generally, there are three layers to consider that each fulfill a particular function.

The first layer up against your skin is called *base layer*. It includes your underwear and hiking shirts. The base layer helps control your body temperature by moving perspiration away from your skin, so fabrics with excellent moisture-wicking capabilities are highly preferable. The next layer, called *middle layer*, provides insulation to help retain heat by trapping air close to your body. A light merino sweater or fleece jacket are suitable options for the LSHT. Both are breathable and insulate even when wet. If very cold temperatures are to be expected, consider packing a puffy down jacket. It offers the best warmth-to-weight ratio and is highly compressible. Spending a little more money on water-resistant down is advisable.

 If possible, pick shirts and jackets without seams on the shoulders to avoid rubbing and pressure points from your pack straps.

The outer layer, called *shell layer*, provides protection from wind and rain. Shells are categorized (and priced) based on their properties regarding water-resistance and breathability. Since it is quite possible for heavy rain and high temperatures to occur simultaneously on the LSHT, your ideal shell will be both waterproof and properly ventilated to let perspiration escape. However, choices that combine the best of both worlds are rather costly. Finding a more economical alternative will likely require compromising on either property. Proper fit is another consideration as your shell layer should be roomy enough to fit easily over other layers and not restrict your movement.

In summary, it is advisable to be prepared for all eventualities by packing both light and airy clothes as well as weatherproof and warm layers.

Additional Clothing

Whether to wear shorts or light hiking pants on the trail is a matter of personal preference. Pants keep dirt off your legs and provide additional protection. Shorts are cooler and generally less restrictive. Convertible pants offer the most flexibility as lower legs can be easily taken off and put back on using zippers.

In addition, most hikers will opt for some form of headgear – a brimmed hat, visor, base cap, hat with neck flap, or other. While sun protection is nice to have, it is not a major concern on the LSHT given the fact that trees provide adequate shade. Rather consider an option that will keep your head warm and your face dry during windy and rainy conditions. An insect net that goes over your head and headgear offers additional protection.

Consider bringing flip-flops, sandals, or other light footwear to wear at camp. Knowing you can take your shoes off after a long day of hiking becomes ever more appealing with every mile traveled. Opt for a light-weight, water-repellent or, at least, quick-drying option that could also be worn when taking a shower.

You may want to consider bringing a pair of long pants for the evenings, if nothing else but to protect your legs from mosquitoes. Then, in your sleeping bag, long underwear bottoms and a long-sleeved top are best suited to keep yourself warm and your sleeping bag clean. A beanie and/or scarf can provide additional warmth during particularly cold nights.

Washing Clothes

There are limited options for washing clothes along the LSHT. Your best bet are probably the restrooms at developed campgrounds. Try to avoid washing clothes in natural streams and ponds to minimize the impact on the environment and entirely refrain from using non-biodegradable detergents. Drying clothes can be challenging, especially during months with high humidity levels. Clothes with less pockets and zippers tend to dry faster and are less likely to damage each other during washing.

Example Clothing List

This was my clothing pack list for the LSHT:

2 pairs of hiking socks	1 fleece jacket
2 underwear	1 rain shell
1 hiking pants w/ detachable legs	1 visor
2 long sleeve shirts w/ high zip collar	1 beanie (night)
1 turtleneck shirt (night)	1 long underwear (night)
1 t-shirt (night)	1 pair of flip-flops

b. Hiking

Basic hiking gear usually consists of appropriate footwear, additional ankle and leg protection, a fitting and well-balanced backpack, and optional trekking poles. This section provides an overview of available options and features, discusses pros and cons, and offers advice on how to carefully choose and properly fit individual items.

Shoes & Boots

Undoubtedly the most stressed piece of gear on your trip will be your shoes. Suitable models will have thick, cushioning soles with non-slip tread. Additional criteria are ankle support, protection, water resistance, breathability, weight, as well as overall fit and comfort. There are three typical styles – hiking boot, hiking shoe, and trail runner – that each have their individual assets and drawbacks as outlined below.

Hiking Boots provide the most stability overall. A well-fitting boot is snug, supports the ankle, and reduces the risk of twisting on a slight misstep. With more contact area, the foot is less likely to move back and forth. The high rising sides offer additional ankle protection and prevent sand/dust from entering the boot. Another advantage is the high water resistance which may be desirable along the rather muddy sections of the LSHT. Drawbacks of hiking boots are the greater weight, stiffness (and hence resistance during walking strides), chances of blisters from ill-fitting boots, and lower breathability.

Hiking Boot   Hiking Shoe   Trail Runner

Figure 11 – Hiking Shoes & Boots[5]

Hiking Shoes combine the grip and stability of a good boot with more flexibility. The low cut allows more mobility and light mesh uppers enable moisture wicking. Look for firm heel support and a plastic cap to protect your toes. Different brands have various lacing systems, some of which enable great fit in minimal time. Hiking shoes are lighter than boots and generally feel less restrictive while still providing sufficient stability. Drawbacks are reduced ankle support, reduced water resistance, and incompatibility with crampons, although the latter is irrelevant for the LSHT.

Trail Runners go one step further regarding agility and light-weight features, weighing about as much as conventional running shoe. In order to save weight, trail runners usually provide less cushioning than hiking shoes, while still offering good tread and lots of grip. Upper materials are mostly breathable, light meshes, offering more support than running shoes but far less than a boot. Quick lacing systems are also available. Generally, trail runners are aimed at people going for a run in the mountains or woods, not necessarily for long hiking trips with heavy backpacks. Drawbacks are low overall support and cushioning as well as minimal protection and water resistance.

Whichever shoe or boot you decide to go with, make sure you are confident about your choice. It should provide adequate support to you

---

[5] Sketches of Asolo boot and Salomon shoes

and your pack weight, wick moisture away from your feet, not be too heavy and tiring, have a well-cushioned sole, and most importantly a padded inside that does not cause blisters.

(i) Buy shoes at least half a size bigger than you normally would. This will allow you to wear padded socks for additional comfort and prevent your toes from hitting against the tips when descending.

It is strongly recommended to use your new shoes on a few training hikes to break them in and to see how they feel overall. If in doubt, try another pair – getting your shoes right is essential. Also, refrain from wearing shoes that are too worn down and only have little tread left as it will increase the chances of slipping and falling.

Socks & Gaiters

A good sock can significantly add to your hiking comfort. Most modern trail socks are made of merino wool or polyester. Both fibers have outstanding properties regarding moisture wicking and temperature regulation. Thick socks, especially those with hidden seams, provide cushioning and help the shoe embrace your foot evenly, reducing rubbing and blisters. Though less stylish in a shoes-shorts combo and slightly warmer, socks that go (well) above your ankle collect less sand and stones, keep your legs cleaner, and provide better protection from pointy shrubs, poison ivy, and tick bites.

Another option to protect your feet and lower legs are gaiters. They wrap around your ankles or calves and cover the gap between socks and footwear. There are different types of gaiters to choose from depending on the nature of the trip and the conditions expected. Very suitable for the LSHT are trail gaiters. They are the most lightweight, breathable option, offering basic protection against rocks, grit, and light rain.

Compression socks can be of use especially to those who have issues with blood clots, edema, and thrombosis. Compression socks come in different lengths, from knee- and thigh-high, to full pantyhose style. There are different compression gradients to assist circulation. Lower gradients are usually prescription free while higher gradients may require consultation.

In any case, if you are aware of a condition and/or over 40 years old, it is advisable to consult with your doctor to determine whether or not compression socks are appropriate.

Backpacks

There is a multitude of backpack styles, capacities, and functionalities available in the market. Similar to other gear items, finding the right model depends on the nature of your trip and personal preference. In any event, it is important to find one that matches your personal physique. Given the extra weight you will be carrying, an ill-fitting backpack can cause considerable pain, e.g., chaffing along straps and/or back aches from a too restrictive fit. Below is a list of decision criteria to help find a pack that is right for you:

Criteria	Comment
Size	<table><tr><td>Size</td><td>Torso [inch]</td><td>Torso [cm]</td></tr><tr><td>Extra Small</td><td>up to 15 ½</td><td>up to 40</td></tr><tr><td>Small</td><td>15 ½ - 17½</td><td>40 – 45</td></tr><tr><td>Medium</td><td>17½ - 19½</td><td>45 – 50</td></tr><tr><td>Large</td><td>19½ and up</td><td>50 and up</td></tr></table> These are commonly used sizes (learn how to measure your torso further below). Some packs also come in different hip sizes – measure at the widest part. Apart from the (vertical) torso size, the design and cut varies on packs and shoulder straps, making them more or less comfortable for broad- or narrow-shouldered people. Compare and try different packs.
Capacity	Typical packs used to thru-hike the LSHT have capacities of 65-80 liters (all packing capacity is measured in liters and for the medium size). Small and large sizes can vary by +/- 3 liters. While you want to choose the smallest capacity to save weight, you also need to fit all of your gear. The right

	capacity for you depends on how bulky your big items are, i.e., tent, sleeping bag, and pad, and how much and which clothing you plan to bring. Packs allow some flexibility by raising the top lid or strapping a tent or foam pad to the outside. However, this may mean that weights are not optimally distributed. See Section *'Pack & Adjust your Pack'* below for details.
Weight	As with most other gear, the weight of a backpack is closely linked to comfort and price. Thick, comfortable padding along shoulder straps and hip belts adds to the scale. However, keep in mind that you will be carrying this pack all day for an extended period of time, so increasing the weight by adding additional comfort may be worthwhile. The durability of materials also affects the pack's weight. Light packs usually have very thin shell materials that require more caution with handling. They may also be less water-resistant than packs that are more rugged. For the LSHT, it is certainly advisable to consider a more rugged, water-resistant option.
Padding	The padding of shoulder straps, hip belt, and backside of the pack is the essential factor for how you perceive the comfort of a pack, especially when filled with up to 40lbs. Using an ultra-light backpack saves extra weight, but make sure you are comfortable with the limited padding and potential rubbing/chaffing when the pack is loaded and you are in normal hiking motion.
Adjustability	Most modern internal frame packs are very similar regarding their adjustability. Shoulder straps and hip belts can be adjusted in length; load lifter straps connect the pack's top to the shoulder straps and keep the weight balanced near your center; sternum straps connect the shoulder straps across the chest to tighten the pack's fit and increase stability. Some packs have

	an adjustable suspension, meaning the entire shoulder harness system can be slid up and down to customize the pack to the exact torso length. Compression straps along the sides and front of the pack pull the weight close to your center and keep contents from shifting on difficult trail sections. Daisy chains[6], elastic straps, or karabiners allow you to arrange and adjust gear on the outside of the pack.
Compartments	Having certain compartments may not be a key decision factor, however, having a well thought-out design can make trail days easier. Some hikers may insist on a sleeping bag compartment at the bottom of the pack, others may look for a certain number of side pockets to organize and access their content, and still others may want one or two water bottle pockets if that is their chosen hydration strategy. Having a multitude of compartments may facilitate pack organization, however, it may also conflict with a minimalist, ultra-light approach.
Ventilation	A well-ventilated back area with airy padding is a big plus, especially on the LSHT. Proper ventilation adds to your overall comfort, and a dry back and shoulders are also less susceptive to chaffing. Different brands and models have various approaches on how to wick moisture and heat from in-between your back and your pack. Some have air channels between padding, others completely separate the pack from the hiker's back with a tension mesh. Some ventilation methods are more effective and/or comfortable than others. Try them out to find the one that works best for you.

---

[6] Some packs offer a series of external stitched loops called "daisy chain". They are usually placed up along the center of the pack.

Hydration	A standard feature of most packs and worth asking about: a clip inside the pack to hang the hydration pack and an opening to lead the drinking tube to the front.
Frame	There are two frame styles: internal and external frames. Most modern backpacks have internal frames sewed into the pack. Traditionally, packs only had external frames, with large aluminum tubes extending above and around the pack.
	Advantages of the external frame packs are low cost, light weight, and easy packability of bulky items (esp. on the outside). Disadvantages are their limited adjustability and fit, they are less stable on uneven terrain, and they are usually less water resistant.
	Internal packs make up for the above disadvantages, but are usually more expensive and heavier.
Rain cover	A built-in rain cover, usually located in the top lid or at the bottom of the pack, can be wrapped around the entire backpack with an elastic trimming. They are very practical, especially on the LSHT. If it does not come as a standard feature, be sure to obtain a fitting cover for your pack separately.

Table 12 – Backpack Decision Criteria

At times, hikers will be subject to rather challenging conditions on the LSHT. Thus, my recommendation is to opt for a more rugged and weatherproof backpack rather than the most light-weight model. A rain cover is definitely a must-have.

Excursion – Measuring your torso length:

1. Locate your 7th cervical vertebra (C7) at the base of your neck by tilting your head forward. It is the bony bump at the end your vertical spine as your neck is leaning forward. When you run your fingers down your neck, you will first feel the smaller C6 and then C7. This marks the top of your torso.
2. Locate your iliac crest at the top of your hip bone by placing your hands high on your hips. With your thumbs in the back, dig into your pelvis to find the rounded, highest point of your hip bone. The imaginary line between your thumbs marks the bottom of your torso.
3. Measure between top and bottom of your torso. Be sure to stand straight. Assistance while handling the tape measure is helpful.

Pack & Adjust your Pack

As you pack your backpack, pay attention to two things: the weight distribution and the internal organization of your gear.

Regarding weight distribution it is important to keep heavy items close to your back and centered, both vertically and horizontally (see Figure 12). Moderately heavy items should be placed around the heavy items, light ones along the perimeter of the pack (e.g., placing your sleeping bag in the bottom compartment). The goal is to bring the weight in the backpack as close to the center of your back as possible. This way, the pack's center of gravity is closest to your own, making it less likely for you to lose your balance.

A well-considered internal organization and distribution of gear among the compartments and pockets of your pack can save time and nerves. Gear that will only be used once at camp in the evening can be placed inside and below heavy items. Tent poles can also be separated from the tent pack for better storability. Depending on the specific partitioning of your pack, you will see during the first days of hiking which compartments are best suited for what gear. It then helps to stick to a specific organization.

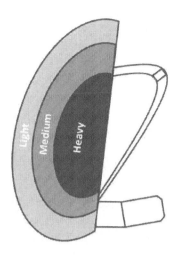

Figure 12 – Backpack Weight Distribution

For easier organization in the main compartment, it is good to use thin plastic bags or (water-resistant) compression sacks. They can be individually stuffed and make accessing contents more convenient while providing additional protection against water and dirt. Valuables (phone, keys, money, etc.) can be kept in a zip lock bag and buried deep, as they will hardly be needed. Keep rain gear easily accessible. Once you have all your items in place and are ready to take off, pull all compression straps. They are usually located on the sides of your pack and at the top. Tightening the compression straps brings the weight closer to your back and prevents gear from shifting.

> [!] Anything that needs easy and frequent access, such as a map, sunscreen, snacks, or a pocket knife, should be stored in an accessible outside pocket near/on the top.

Adjusting your pack starts by putting it on correctly. If your pack is heavy, place one foot forward and lift the pack onto your thigh. Then, slip into the shoulder straps and lean forward, pulling the pack onto your back. As you lean forward, position the pack so the hip belt is centered comfortably over your hip bone, then close and tighten the hip belt firmly. As you straighten yourself up, your shoulder straps should be loose and 100% of the pack's weight on your hips. In this starting position the shoulder straps should have a gap of approx. one inch over your shoulders (however, the anchor points of the shoulder harness will be below your shoulders). If the straps already put pressure on your shoulders in the starting position and your pack has an adjustable suspension, slide the entire shoulder harness up a little and re-secure it. Now, tighten your shoulder straps so they touch your shoulders.

Unlike traditional backpacks, today's packs are supported primarily by the hip belt with only approx. 10% of the weight being carried by your shoulders. Keep this in mind as you adjust and tighten the straps. Then, pull your load lifters (which extend from the top of your shoulder straps to the top of your pack) so that they form a 45-degree angle to a horizontal axis. This brings the pack's center of gravity closer to yours. Now, close your sternum strap and tighten comfortably in front of your chest. This reduces the pack's tendency of pulling your shoulders back. Finally, check your shoulder straps again. The shoulder straps should not be under great tension. Make sure you are merely guiding the weight and keeping it close to your center of gravity rather than carrying it with your shoulders.

Trekking Poles

Section 5b *Training* offered some advice on how to correctly use trekking poles. They can be of great service both for propulsion and providing a sense of security on difficult stretches of trail. Below is some advice on what to look out for when purchasing trekking poles:

- Good fit of grip and wrist strap: avoid sweaty grips (cork is favorable) and chafing straps
- The length of the pole should be easily adjustable
- The locking mechanism (twist or external lever) as well as the overall pole should be sturdy
- The lighter the pole, the better – lighter weight facilitates correct use and is less exhausting
- Shock absorbers can be useful but are mostly a matter of taste – try them out

- Rubber tips absorb shock and muffle impact noise; they provide more grip on rock, less on soft subsoil

c. Sleeping

Putting together an adequate sleep system is an important task to ensure your body gets enough rest to recover from a demanding day of hiking and to prepare for the miles ahead. Commonly used sleep systems consist of some form of shelter, a sleeping bag, and a sleeping pad. Finding the right compromise between personal comfort needs and practical considerations can be challenging. The below overview of common sleep system options will aid your decision making.

Shelters

The four most common shelter options are tent, bivy, hammock, and sleeping under the stars/using a tarp. For couples hiking the LSHT, sharing a tent may be the most convenient and comfortable option. If you are accompanied by a hiking buddy, the benefits of having separate sleeping arrangements may exceed the actual weight savings of sharing.

Tent

A tent provides the most space for you to dress and move around inside as well as for keeping your gear sheltered. Remember, not only rain but also condensation, especially in close proximity to lakes and rivers, will settle overnight and can soak your gear. If the weather is rainy, windy, or just unpleasant in general, quickly pitching your tent and jumping inside provides instant protection and comfort. Getting food ready while taking a look at the map inside can be quite cozy, too. While the lightest single person models weigh only around 2lbs, carrying a tent is one of the heaviest options for shelter. Most modern tents use thin fabrics in order to save weight. Bringing along a footprint, a sheet that is placed under the tent, may be worthwhile as it protects against moisture and punctures from underneath. However, it will also add additional weight.

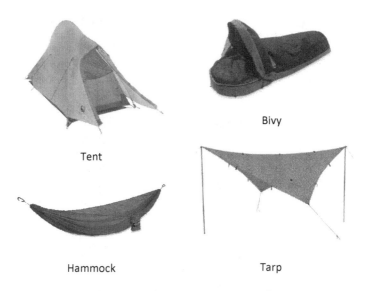

Tent

Bivy

Hammock

Tarp

Figure 13 – Sleeping Shelter Options[7]

Bivy

A bivouac sack, commonly known as "bivy", is slightly bigger than a sleeping bag. The sleeping bag slides into the bivy, which is made of water and wind resistant material. A bivy sack has a small hole or breathable fabric in the head area which can either be left open or zipped shut. The head area generally also features a little dome, providing some extra space to rest on your elbows inside. While bivies offer similar insulation and protection from the elements as tents, inner condensation is a greater problem, because it gets in direct contact with the sleeping bag and has less air circulation. Also, bivies offer no additional space for gear or extensive movement, and people with claustrophobia may not appreciate the confined space.

Hammock

In areas with ample trees of sufficient strength, hammocks are a great alternative to the 1-person ground systems described above. Their construction is independent from underground surfaces and slopes, so

---

[7] Tent: Big Agnes; Bivy: Outdoor Research; Hammock: ENO; Tarp: Kelty

there is more flexibility in choosing campsites. When properly set up using wide tree-straps, hammock systems have a lower impact on vegetation versus pitching a tent or tarp on forest soil. Advocates state that hammocks are more comfortable than grounds systems, however, individual perceptions may vary based on the preferred sleeping position. In combination with a rain fly, hammocks are great solution in wet conditions, keeping you and your gear dry well above moist ground and puddles. On the downside, hammock campers are more sensitive to cooling from underneath, especially if there is wind, and hence, additional insulation may be required (e.g., down under-quilt or foam padding). In areas with lots of bugs, a mosquito net may be another useful addition. Basic hammocks with no extras may help save pack weight, a complete hammock system, however, can weigh just as much if not more than a standard ground system.

Under the Stars/Tarp

To anyone counting ounces, a tent or even bivy may sound like tons. The ultimate ultra-lightweight option is to sleep directly under the open sky, also known as "cowboy camping", sacrificing a good amount of comfort and protection. Selecting an appropriate campsite is paramount with this approach. Tree canopies and dense shrubbery may provide some protection from the elements. A step up from this minimalist approach would be a simple tarp tied at 3-4 corners. However, tarps will rarely be as good a wind deflector or as insulating as a tent or bivy. So when choosing this alternative, make sure your sleeping bag is adequately equipped to defy not only the common weather conditions in Sam Houston National Forest but also its nocturnal inhabitants.

During my trip on the LSHT, I used a single person tent with footprint and was very content with my decision. The footprint was actually an 8x4ft tarp which prevented dampness and cold air from creeping into my tent at night. The tarp also doubled perfectly as additional rain protection for the tent when needed. The sleeping bag/sleeping pad combo I used was quite adequate and very comfortable. As additional insulation, I spread a silver emergency blanket beneath my sleeping pad. I appreciated being able to keep my belongings inside the tent and un-/packing in a dry environment inside.

Sleeping Bags

Sleeping bags come in an overwhelming variety of styles and qualities. It is all the more important to understand which features are relevant for the adventure at hand and those to come in the future. After all, a sleeping bag is a significant investment that should last for 15+ years.

Warmth, expressed by the bag's temperature rating, is your primary decision factor. Fortunately, there is a standardized warmth measurement that lets you easily compare[8]. Depending on which month you are planning to hike, choose a bag with a comfort zone temperature that is equal to or lower than the average low temperature of that month. For example, average daily lows on the LSHT in January drop to around 40°F, so your sleeping bag should have a corresponding comfort zone. Appropriate comfort zones for the LSHT are usually found among 3-season sleeping bags.

All peak performance sleeping bags use down insulation with fill-powers[9] of 700-900 (the higher the number, the better). Down is breathable and provides incredible loft and resulting insolation for its light-weight, while also compressing well. Additionally, there are new hydrophobic/dry downs that even maintain insulation properties after getting wet and/or repel moisture. Modern synthetic fill materials mimic the great properties of down, often at a very competitive price.

Weight is a general concern. Besides the filling, the weight is a function of length, girth, cut, fabric, and features of the sleeping bag. The length is usually a pretty clear decision based on your height. Girth will primarily be determined by your shoulders and belly or hips. Cut refers to the bag's

---

[8] EN Standard 13537: a European Standard for the testing, rating, and labelling of sleeping bags.

[9] Fill-power: a measure of the loft of a down product in cubic inches per ounce; it describes to what volume one ounce of down expands to.

shape: most bags available today are mummy style that follows the contours of the body – wider at the shoulders and narrow along legs and feet. Some bags are cut straight, providing more space but also more material to carry. Fabrics lining the sleeping bag are usually made of light-weight synthetic materials. Features include hoodies, draft tubes[10], zippers, inside pockets, and more. Take a look at different features to find out if you care about any of them in particular. If you don't, cross them off your list of sleeping bag must-haves and save the weight.

Combining the above aspects leads to the warmth-to-weight ratio. This figure compares the bag's temperature rating to its weight. Best ratios are achieved with hood-less, no-frills, down mummy bags that have reduced padding in the back. However, going ultra-light requires some experience, especially on how to substitute certain weight savings on one piece of gear with another gear item that is already part of your essentials. If it requires adding another piece of gear that is non-essential, it defeats the purpose. For instance, the lack of an attached hood on a sleeping bag can be compensated with a hooded down jacket and/or a warm hat, which anyone will most likely pack anyway. The padding in the back, which is compressed when lying on it and, hence, loses its insulating properties, can be reduced if the sleeping pad offers sufficient insulation.

Pack size is another important factor. It correlates strongly with the bag's warmth and weight – unfortunately, also with its price. Everything that reduces the weight usually reduces the pack size. In contrast, warmer bags with more filling typically don't compress as much. Given this trade-off, do not opt for an inadequate comfort zone to reduce compression size unless you have a plan to make up for that loss of warmth.

Fit and feel should be agreeable to provide the most comfort. Materials should feel pleasant and you should have sufficient space around your shoulders, hips, and feet based on your subjective preference. Some people find mummy sleeping bags to be confining, others feel suffocated

---

[10] Draft tube: an insulating flap or tube that covers the zipper to avoid heat loss out of the sleeping bag.

by a draft collar, still others prefer a snug fit. A good outdoor store should have several models for testing – try them and find out which type you are.

Lastly, choosing your sleeping bag must match your choice of camping strategy. If you are sleeping without a shelter, your sleeping bag should be particularly warm, wind- and water-resistant. However, water-resistant shells are less breathable and require more time for your bag to loft. If you plan to save weight on filling and frills by wearing a down jacket, make sure the sleeping bag provides enough inner space for the jacket's loft. In the end, deciding on a particular sleeping bag will be a compromise between choosing desired features and staying within a reasonable budget.

Due to rain and rather high humidity levels on the LSHT, wet or, at least, damp conditions are not uncommon. No matter which style or comfort level you prefer for you sleeping bag, make sure to opt for materials that resist rather than absorb moisture. Treated down, for example, stays dry much longer than untreated down and also dries much faster in case it does get wet. Keep in mind that a dry sleeping bag is not only more comfortable than a damp/wet one, but also much lighter!

Sleeping Pads

A sleeping pad should literally support a good night's sleep. The two main criteria are cushioning and insulation. While forest soil is generally softer and more even compared to the rocky surfaces found in mountainous regions, you can count on the ground being cold and relatively damp along most stretches of the LSHT. There are three popular and equally suitable alternatives:

Air Pads – Similar to the ones used in swimming pools, hiking air pads have a thin air-tight shell that is inflated through a mouth valve. In order to cut down on weight, they are often semi-rectangular in shape. Air pads are generally very light-weight, roll up very small, and offer exceptional cushioning, especially those with a thickness of two inches and up. On the downside, inflating a thick pad may require more than a minute of lung blasting, light-weight models can be noisy due to crackling material, and punctures are a concern.

Foam Pads – Usually made of dense, closed-cell foams, foam pads can either be rolled up or folded like an accordion. They are light-weight, inexpensive, provide great insulation, and are practically indestructible from rough surfaces. On the downside, foam pads are usually not very thick and provide limited cushioning comfort. They also don't compress and, therefore, pack rather large.

Self-inflating foam pads - Combining the packability of an air pad with the cushioning of a foam pad, while needing only little additional inflation. Thin pads are light-weight and compress well into a small sack. On the downside, they offer limited cushioning, while thicker pads of over two inches are rather heavy.

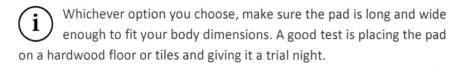 Whichever option you choose, make sure the pad is long and wide enough to fit your body dimensions. A good test is placing the pad on a hardwood floor or tiles and giving it a trial night.

Sleeping Gear

Apart from the clothing you wear in your sleeping bag, there are other gear items that can provide additional comfort, such as a pillow, eye mask, ear plugs, and insect repellent.

An alternative to packing an inflatable pillow is using your sleeping bag's stuff sack as a casing, and stuffing it loosely with clothes. An eye mask can be helpful for light-sensitive people, especially during a bright full moon. Ear plugs are tricky, they are certainly useful if you cannot catch any sleep due to surrounding noises, but wearing them will make you less aware of rodents or larger animals in the vicinity. Insect repellent can come in handy, especially when camping near water and in an open shelter or entirely without.

Lighting in the dark is also important to think about – for camp preparations in the evenings, early or late hiking, reading in the tent, and when nature calls at night. Headlamps are great because you have both hands free which is useful in any of the above scenarios (ensure adequate battery life). Another option are solar lamps which come in an increasing variety. Charging solar devices may pose a challenge on the LSHT because of the extensive tree canopy. In any event, opt for energy-efficient LED light sources and remember to keep your light within reach at night.

d. Food & Water

While Section 5c *Food* discussed the type of food and drinks to bring and send as resupply, this section focusses on various gear items needed to store, prepare, and consume food, as well as to treat and store water.

Stove & Fuel

While campfires may be allowed on the LSHT under certain conditions, they probably help more with improving the ambience than they do with cooking. Camping stoves are a much more convenient and efficient option when it comes to timely meal preparation. There are two common stove fuel systems – gas canisters and liquid fuel – that are usually available at larger department and hardware stores near Sam Houston National Forest.

Gas Canisters

Gas canisters are filled with a pressurized gas mix of isobutene and propane. They have a self-sealing valve at the top and thread. Stoves can be screwed directly onto the tops. The thread securely fastens the stove to the canister, using it as a stand. These stoves are extremely light (<3oz) and pack very small.

Stoves can also be connected remotely. Remote stoves are placed on the ground and connected to the canister via a fuel line. Consequently, the canister can be flipped on its head, also referred to as an inverted canister. Inverting the canister allows operation in liquid feed mode. This way, gas does not (need to) vaporize inside the canister. By avoiding the need for vaporization, the gas can be used at lower (sub-evaporation) temperatures and performance is upheld. Especially in cold conditions, this comes in handy as the output is increased even with only little gas remaining. In addition, placing the stove directly on the ground can also improve pot stability and wind shielding.

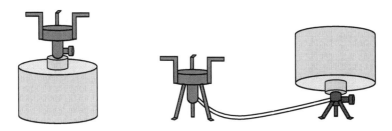

Figure 14 – Canister Stoves: Top and Remote (Inverted) Mounted

The third pressurized gas setup is called an integrated canister system. These systems have an integrated burner and heat exchanger that are directly attached to the bottom of a pot for optimum heat transfer. These compact units are well shielded against wind, and their pots are often insulated against heat loss. Integrated canister systems are especially efficient for boiling water. However, it lies in their nature that they cannot be remotely fed and thus have limited cold weather performance.

Generally, all canister systems are easy and fast to use as they don't require priming. They burn cleanly, reach their maximum heat very quickly, and there is no risk of fuel spillage. On the downside, pressurized gas is rather expensive, and gauging how much fuel is left is difficult. Upright mounted canisters (not inverted) bear the risk of tipping over and struggle with the properties of gas, which leads to limited cold-weather operability and reduced performance as canisters empty.

Excursion – Operating pressurized gas canisters in cold weather – understanding the limits:

The lowest operating temperature of a pressurized gas canister is a matter of its gas composition. Good hiking canisters consist of isobutene and propane, large barbeque canisters often contain n-butane. A canister gas' operating temperature limit is determined by the gas with the highest (warmest) boiling point. Since propane has the lowest boiling point temperature (see Table 13), it will burn off first, especially in an upright canister system.

Boiling Point	° Fahrenheit	° Celsius	Approx. Limit
N-Butane	31	+/- 0	41°F/5°C
Isobutene	12	-11	21°F/-6°C
Propane	-44	-42	-35/-37°C

Table 13 – Boiling Points of Stove Canister Gases at Sea Level

If only n-butane is left, the stove's working limit would be around 41°F, since the stove system needs a certain pressure to operate which requires some thermal energy exceeding the respective boiling temperature to vaporize the gas. Otherwise, at lower temperatures, the n-butane would sit as a non-vaporizing liquid at the bottom of the canister. This explains the positive effect of a liquid-feed stove and inverting the canister. The composition of the liquid gases remain constant, i.e., the gas that is less adequate for cold weather is not left behind to cause the canister to fade when approaching depletion.

The right gas composition is an important selection criterion, especially when cold weather conditions are to be expected. Keep in mind, while temperatures below freezing are not common on the LSHT, they are possible, especially during the winter months. Canister stoves are well-suited for the LSHT, in particular when containing a propane-isobutene mix. With an operating temperature limit of 21°F at sea level, canister stoves will provide reliable heat along the trail. Liquid feed canister stoves offer additional low temperature range.

| ! | Remember, the fuel temperature is key, not the ambient temperature. When confronted with very cold conditions, keep |

your canister inside your tent or even at your feet in the sleeping bag to ensure the gas temperature is a few degrees above its boiling point.

Liquid Fuel

Liquid fuel stoves have a similar setup as remote liquid-fed canister systems. The burner is placed on the ground and connects via fuel line to the bottle fuel tank, which has a pump to pressurize the fuel and a valve to control flow. Most systems require priming, especially in cold conditions. Priming means that a few drops of fuel are placed into a dish underneath the burner and lit. This heats the attached fuel line and causes the fuel to vaporize and push into the actual burner where it can be ignited.

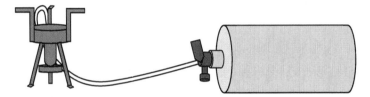

Figure 15 – Liquid Fuel Stove

Liquid fuel systems are dominated by white gas (a.k.a. naphtha). This is a highly refined fuel with little impurities so it burns very clean. There are also multi-fuel stoves that run on white gas, kerosene, diesel, and gasoline. Generally, the greatest advantages of a (petroleum based) liquid fuel stove are the easy international availability of its fuels, their low cost, very high heat output, and their ability to operate at low temperatures. White gas, for example, freezes at −22°F to which the stove is operable. Downsides are that some fuels are odorous, smoke, and may blacken pots. The stoves, especially multi-fuel models, are rather expensive. Flames are not as finely adjustable for simmering foods and overall operation (incl. pumping and priming) needs some practice and bears the risk of flares or burns. Stoves require regular maintenance to avoid clogging, even more so the less purified the fuel is. All this requires some experience and commitment.

Regarding weight, liquid fuel systems are heavier than canisters, due to the more complex burner and pump-valve system for the bottle tanks. Additionally, petroleum fuels have an approx. 5% lower energy density than commonly used pressurized gases. However, liquid fuel tanks are reusable and can be filled as needed, whereas gas canisters can only be bought in a few sizes, making incremental adjustments to fuel supplies difficult.

Fuel Calculation

This leads to the very important question of how much fuel to carry. Unless your meal plan requires special preparation, your fuel consumption will be in direct proportion to how much water you will be boiling per day. A good approximation of how much fuel is needed to boil water is 0.012oz fuel per ounce of water. If certain meals require simmering after the water has boiled, add 0.035oz of fuel per minute of cooking time.

Figure 16 shows the equation used to estimate fuel consumption per trail section, i.e., days until resupply. Remember to consider all your sections, including side trips, and think about which fuel tank sizes or gas cartridges are best suited to provide sufficient energy while minimizing weight.

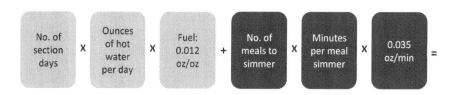

Figure 16 – Estimating Fuel Needs

One example for estimating fuel consumption:

Anna plans to hike the LSHT in eight days without resupplying, so she only needs to calculate fuel consumption for one section. Her estimates for hot water demand per day are as follows:

	8oz	for coffee in the morning
+	8oz	for porridge/oatmeal
+	0oz	for lunch
+	16oz	for a meal in the evening
+	8oz	for one cup of tea
=	40oz	of boiling water per day

Five of her meals each have to be simmered for ten minutes. The rest of her meals are dehydrated/instant meals that don't require simmering. Consequently, her fuel estimate is as follows:

$$(8d \times 40oz \times 0.012oz/oz) + (5d \times 10min \times 0.035oz/min) = 5.6oz$$

Anna needs approx. 5.6oz of fuel for eight days. As a result, one 8oz canister of fuel (gross weight 13.1oz) would suffice for the entire trip and even leave her with some extra fuel.

(i) In order to keep boiling times and wasted fuel low, always use a lid, start on a small flame and increase as water gets warmer, never turning to full throttle. Furthermore, use a screen or heat reflector around your stove and pot to shield the flame from wind.

Lastly, don't forget to bring proper means to ignite a flame. Options include gas lighters, matches, piezo igniters, and spark strikers. Opt for something that is durable, long-lasting, reliable, and water-resistant. It is not recommended to solely rely on only one option. Bring at least one redundant option as a backup in case your first choice gets wet or breaks.

Pots, Pans, and Utensils

Deciding which kind of pot and/or pan to bring depends on your choice of food and the amount of people you will be cooking for. For example, if you are cooking for 1-2 people, one pot with a capacity of approx. 32oz is sufficient. The more liquid the contents are, i.e., soups or water, the better the heat energy circulation and the narrower the pot's base can be. Especially, if you plan on only boiling water during a summer trip, an integrated canister system is the quickest and most efficient way of heating. However, if you intend to prepare solid meals, opt for a pot or pan with a wider base and choose an easy to clean non-stick surface.

In either case, materials such as aluminum or titanium help save pack weight and always using a lid conserves your fuel. Whether the pot or pan has an integrated (foldable) handle or comes with a multi-use detachable one is secondary.

 Another important feature to look for is how well pots and dishes can be stacked inside each other while not in use to save space.

While putting together your meals, it helps to think about and set aside the utensils it will take to prepare them. The standard minimum is usually a spoon or "spork" (spoon and fork in one) and a pocket knife. Long-handled spoons are particularly convenient when eating directly out of the freeze-dried meal pouches or the pot. However, if your meals require stirring or flipping on the stove, make sure your utensil is heat resistant.

Water Treatment

As discussed earlier in the book, it is advised to treat any water from natural sources before drinking. There are six options for doing so: micro-filter pumps, micro-filter gravity and squeeze bags, ultra-violet (UV) sterilization pens, chemical tablets/drops, and boiling. Generally, filters treat protozoa, bacteria, and particles, and allow instant water consumption. Boiling, UV light, and chemical purifiers are effective against protozoa, bacteria, and viruses; however, only if the drawn water is almost clear and after a certain treatment time. All options except pumps are of limited applicability in shallow or small amounts of water. Table 14 below provides an overview of respective capabilities, features, and costs.

On the LSHT, water availability and quality vary greatly based on weather conditions. After periods of rain, you may find streams and ponds to carry sufficient quantities of clear water. During droughts, however, smaller creeks tend to dry up and rivers as well as ponds will only carry low quantities of rather murky water. Personally, I prefer to be on the safer side when it comes to water purification, so my recommendation is to bring along a pump filter to filter out any larger particles before using chemical tablets/droplets or UV-based purifiers.

Feature	Boiling	Chemical	UV Light	Squeeze	Gravity	Pump
Speed [l/min]	0.2	0.1-0.25	0.7-1.0	1.5-1.7	1.4-1.8	1.0-1.6
Weight [oz.]	0.4/l	2-3	4-6	2-5	8-12	10-15
Treats Viruses	yes	yes	yes	no	no	no
Longevity [l]	n/a	80-100	>10k	>10k	1-2k	1-2k
Ease of Use	easy	very easy	easy	medium	very easy	easy
Durability	long	n/a	fair/long	fair	long	fair/long
Cost [$]	40-50 ct/l	10-15 ct/l	80-160	30-50	80-120	80-100
Comment	Requires fuel and drinking hot water	Ineffective in murky water; virus treatment, but >0.5h, slight chemical taste	Ineffective in murky water, requires batteries / charging	Hard squeezing led to pouch tears, hand strength needed	Best if hung, incl. storage bags, great for groups	Pre-filter filters large particles, requires maintenance

Table 14 – Water Treatment Options

Similar to other gear items, choosing an appropriate water treatment system is a trade-off. Below is a summary of the key takeaways from the overview table to support you with your decision:

- Pump filters are fast and work well even in little, murky water, but they are rather heavy and require some maintenance.
- Gravity filters are fast, very easy to use, and the clean tank can double as a hydration pack, but they are expensive and rather heavy.
- Squeeze filters are fast, light, cheap, and filter large amounts of water per cartridge (life span of over 10,000 l/cartridge), but the squeezing is strenuous and the pouch can easily tear or puncture if squeezed too hard.
- UV lights often come as a pen or integrated in a bottle. They are light, rather fast, and treat viruses, but they rely on batteries to work and somewhat clear water to be effective.
- Chemical options are chlorine dioxide, sodium dichloroisocyanurate, and iodine tablets or droplets. They are very light, cheap, and treat viruses, but slower than other options and less effective in murky water. Plus, a slight chemical aftertaste usually remains. Also, the individual tablet dosage should match your drinking container size. Some tablets are for two liters of water and hard to break. In case your container has a different volume, droplets are an alternative.
- Boiling water can only be a backup option. It is slow, heavy (incl. the fuel needed), and leaves you with hot water to quench your thirst in warm conditions.

Water Storage

It is also worth putting some thought into how to store the treated water for convenient and frequent access. Two options are most common – water bottles and hydration packs.

Practical *water bottle* sizes are 24-48oz. Aluminum, stainless steel, and BPA-free plastic are the most used and suitable materials. Features like narrow or wide openings, sealing valves, and straws are up to personal preference. Insulated bottles are also available but generally heavier and have less capacity. Bottle caps with loops allow attaching to the backpack with a karabiner.

Hydration packs consist of a reservoir made of puncture-resistant, durable material that is placed inside your backpack and a connected drinking tube through which fluids are consumed. A bite valve at the end of the drinking tube helps control the fluid flow. The tube can be clipped onto your backpack strap or lapel for easy access when not in use. Typical sizes of reservoirs are 67-100oz. Wide openings ease filling and cleaning of the packs. Built-in loops at the top allow hanging of the reservoir inside the backpack.

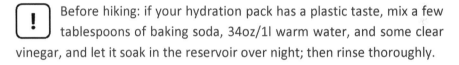 Before hiking: if your hydration pack has a plastic taste, mix a few tablespoons of baking soda, 34oz/1l warm water, and some clear vinegar, and let it soak in the reservoir over night; then rinse thoroughly.

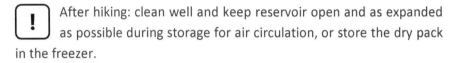 After hiking: clean well and keep reservoir open and as expanded as possible during storage for air circulation, or store the dry pack in the freezer.

Choosing the right water storage and hydration system is a matter of personal preference and hiking strategy. When using trekking poles, for example, a hands-free drinking option may be preferable. Also, the easy access may encourage to drink more frequently and, consequently, reduce the chance of dehydration. A large reservoir will get you far and storing it in your backpack helps distributing the weight evenly on shoulders and hips. The only downside is having to remove the reservoir from your backpack for refilling and for gauging your consumption.

This leads to the question of what size your container(s) should be and how much water to carry after each resupply. They average hiker will consume approx. one gallon of water per day, including meal preparation. Depending on how many reliable water sources there are in a given trail section, this amount can be split proportionally to reduce pack weight.

However, keep in mind that the more frequently you plan to resupply, the more often you will have to unpack your treatment gear.

(i) Depending on the chosen capacity for your water bottle or hydration pack, it may be necessary to bring along additional water reservoirs to ensure sufficient supply. There is a variety of collapsible water bottles available that are light-weight and durable.

For completeness sake, don't forget to pack a mug for drinking tea or coffee at camp. I found that an 18oz plastic mug with a "sippy" lid works best to limit spills and keep contents warm. It also doubles nicely as a measuring cup for food preparation.

e. Medical & Personal Care

For light-weight enthusiasts, this section may be particularly painful. It deals with bringing several items of which you hope never to use any. Nevertheless, a well-equipped first aid kit is vital in case of emergency. Your personal kit should include any medications you regularly take, including those that were recommended by your doctor for this specific trip. There are various well-equipped pre-packed first-aid kits, however, hikers tend to have different needs and standards regarding personal care when outdoors. Limit yourself to the minimum you feel comfortable with. Below are some suggestions on what to pack.

First Aid – General

- Self-adhesive bandages
- Tape (sufficient for emergency and blisters)
- Antibacterial wipes/ointments
- Non-stick sterile pads
- Self-adhesive stretch bandage wrap
- Scissors or knife
- Pain relieving gels/creams (with Camphor, Menthol, Arnica)
- Anti-inflammatories and/or pain relievers (e.g., ibuprofen)
- Blister treatment (bandages, pads, etc.)

- Survival blanket (silver/insulated)
- Whistle

First Aid – Specific or Optional

- Any personal medication
- Anti-histamines (to remedy allergic reactions)
- Tweezers (for splinters)
- Safety pins
- Insect-sting relief
- Sun relief (e.g., Aloe Vera)
- Blood thinner (e.g., Aspirin)

Personal Care

- Sunscreen
- Lip balm
- Tooth brush & paste
- Soap (biodegradable)
- Deodorant
- Insect repellent
- Moisturizer

Since most of the trail is rather well-shaded, sunscreen and lip balm may be dispensable items depending on the sun intensity to be expected. Given the high prevalence of mosquitoes, ticks, chiggers, and other biting insects, insect repellent is definitely not a dispensable item on the LSHT. Consider a DEET-containing product for additional protection.

! Before using DEET-based repellents, be sure to familiarize yourself with the pros and cons of their application and proper handling instructions.

f. Other Essentials

The following gear items can be just as important as the ones listed previously. Many choices are purely subject to personal preference.

Gear	Comment
Camera	Consider trade-off between weight and photo quality when deciding between SLR, compact, and smartphone cameras. Bring at least one extra battery pack. Bring more if you plan on taking videos. Small padded camera cases that attach to your hip belt are convenient and allow for quick access.
Compass	Generally not required to follow the LSHT main route. However, essential if you are forced to take the unofficial detour around the East Fork of the San Jacinto River.
Fishing Gear	A line and some lures may suffice, but you can also go all out. Refer to Section 4a *Permits & Regulations* for fishing license requirements.
GPS Watch	GPS watches allow tracking and analyzing of various statistics of your hike, e.g., distances traveled, speed, pace, elevation. They are nice to have, but not essential for navigating.
Money	Bring some cash for taxi fares, campsite fees, vending machines, post cards, emergency, etc.
Rope	Useful to hang clothes, replace a strap on backpack, or as shoe lace. Should not be too thick or heavy.
Satellite-based Emergency Device	Useful to call for help in case of emergency since cell phone service is not reliable throughout Sam Houston National Forest.

Shovel	Useful to bury human waste. Should be light and sturdy.
Solar Charger	There is a variety of compact photovoltaic panels incl. rechargeable battery and (USB) power port available to help charge various electronic devices (lights, smartphones, watches, etc.). Their application in the Sam Houston National Forest, however, may be limited due to extensive shade provided by tree canopies.
Sunglasses	Sporty, tight fit, UV protection, polarization is a plus.
Toilet Paper	1-1.5 rolls per week. Keep a small bottle of hand sanitizer inside the roll.
Towel	Quick drying, synthetic fabric, light-weight.

Table 15 – Other Essential Gear

7. Personal Experience

This chapter describes my personal preparation, travel arrangements, gear items, and experience on the LSHT. It is a summary of considerations and efforts that went into my own 6-day journey in February 2015. The below information is intended to provide inspiration, additional guidance, and reference points for shaping your own trip.

a. Plan

Macro-Planning

Since permits are not required for hiking the LSHT, my two main decision criteria for determining the timing of my trip were favorable weather conditions and the end of hunting season. I ended up choosing the third week of February as both of these criteria were met, and it also worked out great with my other obligations. Since none of my regular hiking friends were available during the chosen timeframe, I decided to hike solo. As a next step, I needed to figure out in which direction I was going to walk the trail. In my opinion, there are no major pros or cons for either direction. Logistics may be a deciding factor depending on your travel strategy. Mine was to fly to Houston (instead of driving the 1,500 miles from San Diego), find a motel close to the trail, spend one night there, then walk the trail, and return to Houston right after finishing to visit friends.

The most convenient motel location appeared to be Conroe as it was about the same distance to either end of the trail from there. Since Cleveland seemed to offer more options in terms of getting back to Houston compared to Richards, I decided to walk the LSHT from west to east. The plan was to take a cab to the Western Terminus, arrange for a shuttle from the Eastern Terminus to Cleveland, and then take a rental car back to Houston from there. Alternatively, I contemplated renting a car for the entire duration of my hike and parking it at one of the termini but concluded that it would be a rather costly option. Especially, since it would still require taking a shuttle from one end of the trail to the other.

Once I had figured out the general timing and direction, I started to make travel arrangements. Picking up the rental car in Cleveland on a weekend was going to be a bottleneck since most rental offices close around noon on Saturday at the latest. I decided to reserve the car for Friday afternoon to have Saturday morning as a backup in case my hike would take longer than expected. Taking into consideration the six days I had estimated to spend on the trail meant that my official start date would be the Sunday prior.

Ultimately, I booked a flight from San Diego to Houston for Saturday, February 14, and a motel in Conroe for the same night. I also reserved a rental car for Friday, February 20, and confirmed that someone from the car rental would pick me up from the end of the trail. As for trail shelters, my plan was to camp along the route, unless severe weather conditions would force me to leave the woods. I planned to spend one night each at Huntsville State Park and Double Lake campground, so I made the necessary reservations as well. All of the above arrangements were made about two months in advance.

Micro-Planning

From planning the long lead items, I already knew that I had six days to complete the trail. Given my tight schedule, I didn't plan to do any side trips other than camping at Huntsville State Park (HVSP). I was confident to be able to complete the majority of the trail in five days but preferred to have an extra day as a buffer. Planning to finish in five days resulted in an average daily mileage of approx. 20 [= (96.5mi for LSHT + 4.4mi for HVSP) / 5 days]. That seemed to be reasonable to accomplish given my fitness level and the relatively flat terrain.

The main drivers in determining my actual daily distances were finding appropriate campsites and the availability of water. To ease my way into the hiking trip, I decided not to walk the full 20 miles on the first day. Instead, I wanted to set up a primitive camp somewhere between miles 16 and 17. A little under 22 miles on the second day would get me to Huntsville State Park, where I planned to spend the night. For day 3, I picked the East Four Notch hiker camp since it is approx. 18 miles from Huntsville State Park. The fourth night, I intended to spend at the Double Lake campground, which translated into roughly 24 miles for that day. The remaining 21.5 miles I decided to split into 14 miles for day 5, to spend the night at Mercy hiker camp, and 7.5 miles for the last day.

Unsure of what the actual water situation was going to be, my default strategy was to carry enough water to last me an entire day (approx. one gallon). Accordingly, I made sure that each section would have at least one reliable water source to resupply at. Less critical but also important to include in the itinerary planning efforts are points of interest and difficult trail sections. They may invite/require to spend additional time, which could reduce the daily distance.

Table 16 below shows a simplified version of my actual itinerary. The only difference to my original plan as described above is that I ended up not spending my last night at Mercy hiker camp but instead four miles earlier at an off-the-trail primitive campsite.

Mile	Destination	Day	Miles
16.2	Primitive camp	1	16.2
35.7+2.2	Huntsville State Park campground	2	21.7
51.3	East Four Notch hiker camp	3	17.8
75.0	Double Lake campground	4	23.7
85.0	Primitive camp	5	10.0
96.5	Eastern Terminus	6	11.5

Table 16 – Personal Itinerary

I used the two-page LSHT overview map available from the LSHT Club website to mark my daily goals along with water sources, points of interest, and difficult trail sections. I also compiled a few notes that would help me navigate through particularly tricky trail sections, including those, where trail markers appeared to be missing. This level of detail proved to be sufficient for the LSHT, no additional maps or instructions were required.

The compact trail guide in Appendix B is a great reference for planning your own LSHT itinerary. Once you have determined your ETD and average daily miles, you can easily find and highlight camping options, water sources, and other important trail details within your daily range to plan individual sections. Once you have finalized your itinerary, you can transfer the key items from the compact trail guide to any map you plan to take along.

Food & Resupply

Nutrition plays a major role in completing the LSHT successfully. In addition to the suggestions given in Section 5c *Food*, here are some personal remarks on the food I brought:

Meal	Comments
Breakfast	For breakfast, I alternated between dehydrated granola in a pouch and two packets of naturally flavored oatmeal mixed with two table spoons of protein powder. Oatmeal and granola are two highly recommended options for breakfast. They are simple to prepare and very nutritious. Both come in different flavors, e.g., strawberry, blueberry, maple, peach, cinnamon apple, cherry. If you want to get creative, you can buy a variety of oats, grains, granola, nuts, seeds, coconut flakes, and dried fruit to make your own muesli variations for each day. Mixing your own muesli allows you to combine a variety of great, nutritious ingredients and precisely control your intake.
Lunch	My lunches consisted of different kinds of canned meat and fish in pouches along with a side of whole grain pita crisps. I found this to be the perfect approach, because preparation took little to no time and I didn't have to use any of my cooking utensils. In addition, both proteins could be refined with spices or small sachets of hot sauce to add flavor.

Snacks	I really enjoyed chocolate protein bars as well as other granola bars in a variety of flavors. Dried apricots, apples, and other fruit are also great, but rather heavy. Almonds and nuts are nutritious and come in different flavors but tend to be rather dry. Bite-size pieces of jerky are great when you crave something more savory. Snacks were an important part of my diet. Having something small to nibble on helped me control my energy level throughout the day and also allowed me to stretch the time between main meals whenever a particular trail section took longer than anticipated.
Dinner	Dinners were as simple as they were great. Prior to the trip, I had bought a few dehydrated meals from different brands and tested them on short hikes. There are far more varieties than days on the LSHT, so you can have a different entree every evening. Preparation was quick and easy, just what I needed after a long day of hiking. The only downside may be the price of the pouches at $7-10 each. However, considering their more than acceptable taste and convenient preparation, it was well worth it and I would highly recommend them.
Condiments	Each morning, I had a cup of pre-mixed instant coffee with creamer and sugar – not necessarily the gourmet option but quite acceptable. In the evenings, I had ginger and herbal teas – a great way to warm up and relax. If you are taking self-prepared meals, consider bringing some extra spices, olive oil pouches, or other seasonings. The dehydrated meals didn't need any additional flavoring, but hot and other sauces added some variety to my lunches.

Table 17 – Personal Food Comments

Overall, I was very happy with my food choices. For trips lasting longer than a week, I would definitely try to add more variety and also look into taking advantage of resupply options, which wasn't necessary for my 6-day trip. As for storage, I was able to fit all my food into one 700 cubic inch bear canister, creating a separate layer for each day's ration. While using a bear canister is not required on the LSHT, I found it to be a very convenient way to keep my food organized and dry. There may be lighter alternatives to achieve the same result, but I figured carrying the extra weight would be a good way to condition myself for trips where it is actually required to store food in approved canisters.

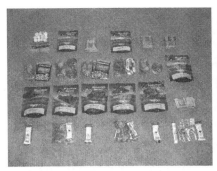

Figure 17 – Organizing Daily Rations and Food Canister

(i) Puncturing freeze-dried meals above the zip lock and letting all air out helps compressing the pouches even smaller to save space.

To give you an example, this is exactly what I packed for my 6-day trip:

Meal	Food	Quantity
Breakfast	Oat meal variations Dehydrated granola	6 packets of different flavors, each mixed with 2 tbsp. protein powder 2 pouches (with milk and blueberries)
Snacks	Granola & protein bars Nuts & dried fruit Beef jerky	12 bars (2 per day) 3 cups (½ cup per day) 6 cups (1 cup per day)

Lunch	Canned meat	4 portions of 4oz
	Fish in pouches	4 pouches of 2.6oz
	Whole grain pita crisps	12 cups (2 cups per day)
	Dehydrated meal	1 pouch of 4oz-6oz
Dinner	Dehydrated meals	5 pouches of 4oz-6oz

Table 18 – Personal Food Quantities

Gear

Assembling gear was a rather simple exercise for me because I already owned most of the required items from previous multi-day hiking trips. When purchasing new gear items, my decision is usually influenced by four main factors (where applicable): pack weight/size, durability, comfort, and price. I find that the happy medium usually works just fine for me. While advocates of ultra-light backpacking may have a different focus, I prefer to own gear that can be used in a range of climates and conditions as different long-distance hikes can vary greatly in nature. The LSHT is a perfect example of a hike where it is probably advisable to lean more towards rugged, weatherproof options rather than focusing too much on ultra-lightweight aspects. Given the sometimes rather unpredictable weather conditions in East Texas, it's probably better to be safe than sorry.

Table 19 below gives you an idea of the gear items I chose for my trip. In hindsight, I would consider my approach to be very average/common for the trail and appropriate for most people's comfort levels.

Gear Item	Comments
Backpack	90l capacity, rather rugged, not the lightest model but very durable, well-padded, and ventilated. Maybe a little oversized, but I prefer to pack everything inside the pack rather than strapping items to the outside. 65-75l could suffice otherwise. I used the sleeping bag compartment for my bear canister – not an ideal weight distribution but very convenient access. Comfortable shoulder straps and hip belt. Many compartments and pockets to organize gear. Separate compartment for water reservoir.
Tent	1-person, 3-season, light-weight tent without footprint (packed weight approx. 3lbs). I highly recommend using a modern, light 1-person tent or hammock over a bivy or tarp. The extra weight is nothing compared to the additional comfort and moving space. If possible, opt for a tent with vestibule space for keeping your gear dry and being able to prepare food during rainy conditions. Since my tent didn't feature a vestibule, I brought a tarp for added rain protection which also doubled as footprint for my tent.
Sleeping bag	700-fill duck down bag with a comfort zone of 20°F. With a pack weight of 2lbs not quite the ultra-light option but very comfortable and warm. Comfort zones of 30-40°F may work as well, but I wouldn't go any higher than that.
Sleeping pad	Ultra-light, inflatable pad. I upgraded from a foam pad and now own a very comfortable air pad that is 2.5in thick and weighs only 12oz – well worth the money.
Stove	Simple, 4-arm-foldout, screw onto canister model – worked great.

Fuel	Gas cartridge with isobutane mix – easy handling, worked great. I used about half an 8oz canister during my trip. I heated water for hot muesli and coffee every morning as well as for tea and dehydrated meals every evening. In general, I try to be conservative with gas consumption by keeping the flame low, the lid on, and using a windscreen.
Lighting device	Spark striker – works great and is absolutely reliable. In addition, I brought a lighter and matches as backup.
Pot	Aluminum pot with a capacity of approx. 34oz. The pot had handles that folded to its sides and a lid. It was inexpensive and absolutely sufficient.
Long spoon/ utensils	Long-handled plastic spoon (ca. 9 inches long). It worked great for scraping muesli out of the pre-packed zip-lock bags and eating straight out of the dehydrated instant meal pouches. That's all I needed.
Bear canister	While not required, I used a 700 cubic in. canister for two reasons: (1) easy food organization; (2) to get used to the extra weight for trails where it is required. I used a transparent model with screw-click lid that worked just fine and doubled perfectly as a seat.
Water treatment	Pump filter system plus iodine drops. I prefer to be on the safer side when it comes to water purification. Water along the LSHT can be rather murky, so filtering out larger particles before using chemical or UV-based purifiers is advisable.
Hydration system	Three 32oz water reservoirs in my backpack plus one 32oz bottle attached to the outside using a karabiner. While not being the best option for drinking during walking, it helps a lot with gauging and controlling water consumption. Refilled external water bottle with water from reservoirs when needed.

Mug with lid	16oz plastic mug with a tight-fitting sippy-cup lid. The mug kept my tea and coffee warm for a long time. Water measuring marks helped with food preparation.
Pocket knife	Swiss army knife with scissors. A knife is a must. Additionally, the scissors came in very handy when cutting tape/bandages.
First aid kit	I compiled my own first-aid kit consisting of antiseptic wipes, bandages, plenty of tape, blister pads, ibuprofen, and arnica gel. Each evening, I applied arnica gel to my knees and ankles to facilitate recovery.
Silver survival blanket	I brought one survival blanket that I spread beneath my sleeping pad for extra insulation. In case of other emergencies or shelter needs, a survival blanket is versatile and weighs little.
Sun protection	Although I had brought sunscreen, I didn't apply it. Wearing long sleeves, high collars, and other textiles is always favorable over sunscreen. Especially, since the combination of dust, sweat, and sunscreen gets ever more uncomfortable throughout the day.
Soap (biodegradable)	One 1oz bottle was more than enough for me. My pot didn't need cleaning since it was only used to boil water, so I only used little soap for cleaning my eating utensils and taking a shower.
Camera	Bringing a SLR camera was no option for me because of its extra weight and bulkiness. Instead, I opted for a point-and-shoot camera, one 32GB SD card, and two extra batteries – all three batteries were empty at the end. The batteries didn't work in the mornings when it was too cold. As a tip, try to keep them in/near your sleeping bag or carry the battery separately in a pant pocket in the morning for quicker warming up. I got a small neoprene case with a belt loop that I attached to

	my hip belt so it wouldn't slide out. This way, my camera was protected and always within my immediate reach. I would highly recommend this approach.
Map	I used the two-page trail map (West & East sections) from the LSHT Club, which I had marked with points of interest, campsites, etc., plus a few notes regarding difficult trail sections and water sources that I had compiled during my research. This level of detail was enough to navigate along the trail.
Money	I didn't plan on making any major resupply purchases along the trail, maybe a few snacks (if any). The only things I envisioned requiring cash for were taxi fares and campsite fees, plus a little extra for emergencies. I spent approx. $100 on cab fare and $40 on camping.
Rope	I brought 15ft of extra, light-weight rope for emergencies. I used it to tie up my backpack for the flight and on the trail for building my front porch on day 2.
Sunglasses	Basic pair of sunglasses with 100% UV protection and polarized lenses. Mainly used during road walking. Within the forest, trees provide sufficient shade.
Head dress	I brought a visor which provided protection from sunlight and also kept rain out of my face. Definitely recommend some form of head dress.
Shovel	Inexpensive, light-weight plastic shovel – sufficed.
Toilet paper	I used only about half a role, mainly because I took advantage of the restroom facilities at campgrounds. Generally, it is a good idea to pack at least one role per week per person. Toilet paper is nothing you would want to have to substitute.

Towel	I brought a medium synthetic, quick drying towel of approx. 18x32in. It is perfectly sufficient for drying off after a shower, and it dries quickly in the wind.
Light source	I brought a battery-powered head lamp which is the most convenient and versatile option for the LSHT in my opinion. I had also packed an LED light with a USB port that connected to my solar charger. While this is generally a viable option as well, recharging can be difficult in the woods.
Trekking poles	As stated earlier, the use of trekking poles is highly recommended. I used extendable telescope poles with twist lock mechanism and cork grips. While these had served me very well during dry conditions on previous trips, the rainy weather on the LSHT definitely took a heavy toll on the lower quality components. The locking mechanism stopped working after a while, and the cork grips began to crumble slowly but surely. I recommend investing a little more in higher quality poles, especially if you plan to double them as tent poles.

Table 19 – Personal Gear Items & Comments

b. Go

Day 0 – Arrival in Houston

I arrived in Houston on Saturday, February 15, one day before my planned start date. During my 3-hour flight from San Diego, California, I met a nice gentleman named Fred who lives and works in College Station, a little town north-west of Houston. We chatted for quite a bit, and when I told him about my upcoming adventure and that I was planning on spending the first night at a motel in Conroe, he offered to give me a lift there without hesitation. Originally, I had planned to take a cab from the airport to the motel, so this noble gesture saved me quite a bit of money. After a quick bite to eat and a spontaneous tour of Houston, Fred dropped me off at my motel near I-45 in Conroe. This was the first, but certainly not the last, indication of how nice and welcoming the people of East Texas are.

Figure 18 – Motel in Conroe and Wrapped Backpack

When I arrived at the motel, it was already later in the afternoon, and I decided to just drop off my luggage and pick up the remaining items for my trip, in particular the fuel for the camping stove. In preparation for that, I had located a shopping center not too far from the motel that featured a number of well-known hardware and department stores which usually carry the fuel canisters that fit my stove. Since it is a very standard item, I trusted that at least one store would have it in stock and didn't call ahead of time to confirm. Big mistake!

When I got to the shopping center, I was unpleasantly surprised to find that none of the stores actually had the fuel canister I needed and given the rather high importance of fuel to prepare food, this quickly turned into a bit of a headache. To avoid having to spend my last evening in civilization roaming around in search of fuel, I decided to look up stores along the route to the trailhead the next day and call them to confirm they had what I needed. I also made sure they would be open early enough since the next day was a Sunday. Taking care of this without additional delays would help me keep my rather tight schedule.

After a few calls, I was fortunately able to locate such store. Phew! I would have never thought that finding a standard fuel canister could turn into such an adventure of its own. Relieved that I had found a solution, I enjoyed dinner at a nearby restaurant and then returned to the motel, where I freed my neatly wrapped backpack and reorganized my gear. I also ordered a taxi that would take me to the LSHT Western Terminus early the next morning. After a last look at the weather forecast, which still predicted a rather high chance of rain for the next days, I went to bed to enjoy what could potentially be the last dry night for a week.

Day 1 – Western Terminus to Stubblefield (16.2 miles)

The taxi picked me up at 7:30am and, including a quick pit stop to pick up the fuel canister, it took us a little over an hour to get to the Western Terminus of the LSHT near Richards. When it came to paying the roughly 100 USD in fare with my credit card, the driver realized that his terminal wasn't working without sufficient cell phone reception. Welcome to the woods! Fortunately, I was prepared for such event and paid him in cash. After filling out the sign-in sheet at the trailhead information board and taking a few "before" pictures, I hoisted my fully-loaded backpack and was on my way. It was a beautiful Sunday morning with perfect hiking conditions. The temperature was in the mid-70s, low humidity, only a few clouds in the sky, and a light breeze blowing gently through the trees.

The goal for the day was to complete the Wilderness and Kelly Section and find a good primitive campsite past mile 16, near Lake Conroe. Large pine trees lined the first stretch of the trail, and evidence of recent prescribed burn activities was showing in the form of partly charred underbrush. Navigating was fairly straightforward due to the abundance of trail markers and signs. I don't think I had to look at my map a single time during the first day. It was such a nice walk through utter woodland solitude, accompanied by singing birds and warm sunbeams shining through the tree tops. You could tell that the area hadn't been receiving a lot of rain recently, because most of the creeks were dried up and ponds only held little water of rather poor quality. Prepared for these conditions and carrying a sufficient supply of water, I enjoyed my lunch sitting on a boardwalk near mile 5, surrounded by dwarf palmetto in a beautiful forest setting.

Figure 19 – Trailhead #1 Information Board and Boardwalk near Mile 5

In the afternoon, clouds started to thicken and a series of medium showers motivated me to get my rain gear out. I ran into a handful of other hikers, two of which actually planned to thru-hike the entire LSHT from west to east as well. A gentleman and his wife, both in their mid-50s, told me their plan was to spend ten days for the entire trip, including two zero days at Huntsville State Park and Double Lake Recreation Area. The rain stopped after approx. two hours, leaving the forest soil soggy and the air damp. Some of the trenches were a bit more slippery now, but overall, the trail was still relatively easy to navigate. The swampy bottomlands near mile 15 made me feel like I was in a jungle, with all the dwarf palmetto, bamboo, hanging vines, and mosses.

Shortly after passing TH#6 and achieving my daily goal, I found a nice, relatively dry primitive campsite surrounded by large loblolly pines. While having dinner, I realized that I hadn't been bothered by a single mosquito all day, probably a nice side effect of the rain earlier. As it started to get noticeably colder around 8:30pm, I retreated into my tent, pulled out my map, and reviewed my plan for the next day. That's when the rain started again.

Figure 20 – Dwarf Palmetto and Nightly Planning

Day 2 – Stubblefield to Huntsville State Park (21.7 miles)

I slept relatively comfortable and well through the night, even though intermittent showers kept tapping against my rainfly. The plan was to get up at around 6:00am, but heavy rain forced me to stay inside my tent for a while longer. When after another hour I realized the rain wouldn't stop any time soon, I pulled out the tarp from underneath my tent and built a little front porch using my trekking poles and the extra rope I had brought. During my various hiking adventures before, I never had to pack up during rain, so it took me a moment to figure out the logistics. The extra 10sqft of covered space certainly helped with moving stuff around without getting it soaked, but the entire process still took quite a while longer than it would have in dry conditions.

Two hours later than originally planned, I finally hit the trail. It was still raining, but after a quick cereal bar and a banana for breakfast, I was ready to conquer the 22 miles planned for day 2. The first stretch to Stubblefield

Campground was rather wet and muddy. It was difficult to tell whether this was the result of the ongoing rain or the close proximity to Lake Conroe – probably both. I stopped at mile 16.5 to enjoy the unobstructed view of Lake Conroe. Without a doubt, it would have been a much more pleasant sight without the rain and thick cloud cover, but I still got an idea as to why it is such a popular spot. Rain and wind made for a rather chilly morning, so I was quite happy to find some shelter in the restrooms at Stubblefield Campground. I used the opportunity to wash up quickly and refill my water reservoirs. The facilities were nice and clean, and the beautifully located waterfront campground with its picnic tables, tent pads, and park-like setting made a very good overall impression.

Figure 21 – Improvised Front Porch and Stubblefield Campground

When I missed the tricky turn shortly after reentering the woods across from Stubblefield overflow camping area (definitely should have paid more attention), it took me a moment before I realized that I hadn't seen a trail marker in a while. Foolishly telling myself that this was probably just one of the less frequently marked sections of the trail, I kept walking, trusting to find more trail markers eventually. However, when the trail I was walking on abruptly ended near a smaller settlement that should theoretically not have been there, it became clear that I had officially wandered off the main route. Looking at my notes, I quickly realized where I had missed the turn, but I wasn't the least bit inclined to walk all the way back. Instead, I waved down a gentleman in his truck who luckily happened to be familiar with the LSHT route. Without hesitation, he offered to give me a ride to the next trail intersection and much to my relief, less than two miles later we were already there. Turns out it actually hadn't been that bad of a detour.

I had already accepted the fact that I would arrive at Huntsville State Park much later than planned, but it was important to reach the spillway at Camelia Lake before nightfall in order to cross it safely. While the rain let up in the afternoon, the temperature remained chilly. I walked along frequently changing vegetation, past ferns and palmettos, hanging vines, shrubbery, and the highest elevation point of 400 feet near mile 31. When I finally got to Camelia Lake, the sun had just begun to set – perfect timing. Although the water was only about an inch deep, the surface of the spillway was pretty slippery. Luckily, the increased stability from using my trekking poles helped prevent any circus-worthy stunts.

Figure 22 – Highest Elevation and Camelia Lake Spillway

After crossing the spillway, it got dark very quickly and I still had quite a ways to go. The warm shower at Huntsville State Park dangling in front of me like a carrot, I pulled out my headlamp and marched through the swampy bottomlands of Alligator Branch. It was a very interesting experience walking through the woods at night, listening to random noises in the distance, and watching fog arise from swamps and ponds on both sides of the trail. This setting in combination with the meager light from my headlamp somehow reminded me of the movie Blair Witch Project from the late 1990s. At that point, however, I was already way too tired to worry about falling victim to sorcery. After two more hours of walking in auto pilot mode, I finally arrived at Huntsville State Park. Rather exhausted but happy to have completed the 21+ miles section despite the late start, I zipped up my sleeping bag at around 10:00pm.

Day 3 – Huntsville State Park to East Four Notch Hiker Camp (17.8 miles)

Tuesday morning I allowed myself a little more time to get ready. I enjoyed an extended breakfast overlooking Lake Raven and read up on all the different activities the park has to offer. Huntsville State Park is very beautiful and well-worth the side trip from the LSHT. I would have enjoyed exploring the area a little longer but needed to get going eventually. The air in the morning was very fresh and crisp. The sky was partly cloudy and a cold breeze motivated me to add another layer of insulation.

Fortunately, there was no sign of the potential thunderstorm the weather forecast had predicted with 40% probability for that day so far, and I was hopeful it would stay that way. After leaving the park and crossing under the I-45, I was walking along the road when a police car pulled over. The sheriff and his deputy asked me how I was doing and where I was headed. After a brief chat about the weather and my LSHT hike, they wished me good luck and continued on. Another example of how friendly and welcoming people in the area are, I thought.

Figure 23 – Forest Setting and Truck on Rails

After lunch, the weather got even better. For most of the afternoon, I walked under a clear blue sky with lots of sunshine. The warmth felt great after the rather chilly morning and the cold and wet conditions the day prior. It is such a different experience hiking the LSHT during nice weather as colors become much more vibrant and wildlife activity in the forest increases noticeably. In addition, my legs felt really good considering the long and strenuous day before. Shortly after turning on Four Notch Road past mile 42, I approached the rail road tracks and the bars were closed.

Much to my surprise, it was not a train that was approaching but a pickup truck. In addition to its regular wheels with rubber tires, it was fitted with flanged steel wheels for running on rails. While this may be a totally normal thing for many people, I had never seen one of these so-called "road-rail vehicles" before and was pleasantly surprised. I continued to walk past historic ranches and open farmland during perfect weather, which was just gorgeous and a nice break from the occasional monotony of the thick woods.

Figure 24 – East Texas Farm and Sunset Shadows

As I was walking along the little country road, a gentlemen who was about to pull out of his driveway stopped, rolled down his window, and asked me: "You doin' the trail?". "Yes!", I replied. And he responded: "It's a good day for it!" – I couldn't have agreed more. Looking around and thinking about how much these little things add to the overall charm of the LSHT, I almost missed the turn onto Forest Service Road 213. When I reentered the woods at trailhead #8 (start of Four Notch section), the forest setting was equally picturesque. The blue sky formed the perfect background for the vibrant, green tree crowns, and when the sun began to set, tall trees threw long shadows on the forest floor. At mile 48, I passed the traditional half-way point of the LSHT. Shortly after, I reached Boswell Creek which was relatively easy to cross. Its water was remarkably clear, probably due to the sandy underground.

As daylight faded, the forest became very lively. More birds starting to sing, some serious wood pecking was going on, and owls hooted at the slowly rising moon. The Four Notch Section seemed to be the most active stretch up to that point. I arrived at the East Four Notch hiker camp just before it got dark. The designated campsite was surrounded by large trees, so before pitching my tent, I made sure none of them looked dead or were leaning towards me. Since there was still no cloud in sight, I enjoyed dinner under a beautiful, starlit sky. It was the perfect end of a wonderful hiking day and a great reminder of why camping in the outdoors is such a grounding and rewarding experience.

Day 4 – East Four Notch Hiker Camp to Double Lake Rec. Area (23.7 miles)

At 6:00am, I got woken up by an overly ambitious rooster. Throughout the night, I had also heard dogs barking on and off, so the campsite couldn't have been too far from civilization. With 24 miles on my agenda for the day (to get to Double Lake Recreation Area), I wasn't too unhappy about the additional encouragement to get up early. It was also the day I would have to face the LSHT's biggest obstacle, the San Jacinto River East Fork. While conditions didn't look too bad when I had left, I didn't know how much the recent rain would have changed that. Getting there before sunset was definitely going to be a challenge, but also crucial in order to allow for safe passage. So after a quick breakfast, I hoisted my backpack and got going while the sun was starting to make its ascent towards the tree tops.

That morning, for the first time, I had to resupply water from a natural source. I had chosen the off-trail pond near mile 58.5 and was pleased to find that the water there was rather clear and plentiful. It was another beautiful morning in the woods with a clear sky and fresh air. Shortly after turning right onto Forest Service Road 207, I spotted a dark object amidst the high grass near the road in the distance. First, it looked like a large tree stump, but when I got closer, I saw vapor arising from the grass. That's when it started to dawn on me that it must be an animal, most likely a feral hog, as I had seen plenty of evidence of their activity on the trail the day before. I snuck up closer and it was indeed a feral hog. Unfortunately, when I tried to get a picture of the bristled fellow, it must have scented me and took off into the woods.

Figure 25 – Pond near mile 58.5 and John Warren Road

The following forest section and even the 2-mile stretch on John Warren Road were very pleasant to walk on and offered a rich variety for the attentive eye. The gorgeous weather certainly helped. At around 1.30pm, I arrived at the Evergreen Baptist Church and used their outside tap to top off my water reservoirs. The following 2.6 miles on FM 945[11] turned out to be my least favorite stretch of the LSHT, despite the beautiful weather. It's mostly uphill walking along a rather busy road with very limited visual stimulation. Unless you are absolutely adamant about walking every single mile of the LSHT (like I was), I highly recommend trying to hitchhike this stretch as it is really more of a chore than a pleasure. In retrospect, that's

---

[11] FM is short for "farm-to-market", a state or county road that connects rural or agricultural areas to market towns.

what I should have done, too. Once you reenter the woods at TH#10 on Butch Arthur Road, the scenery changes for the better again. I took a minute to inspect LSHT hiker camp #2 and it made a really good impression, featuring a tent pad, fire pit, and a few fallen tree trunks that served as seating.

From there, it was about 2.5 miles to get to the infamous East Fork of the San Jacinto River. With every step, my anticipation rose more as to what the conditions would be like when I got there. I was mentally prepared to wade through waist-deep water and had also printed out the directions for the unofficial detour if worse came to worst. It was actually a very beautiful hike through a region of mature Southern magnolia trees that surround the bottomlands of the San Jacinto River.

I made it to the East Fork right before the sun started to set. Much to my relief, the water level was rather low (about three feet). After a quick look at the remains of the old bridge, I further examined the west bank of the river to locate the best spot for crossing. Much to my delight, I came across a few logs that had been strategically placed to form a small footbridge. The logs were rather slippery so I decided to remove all heavy and sturdy items from my backpack and to throw them across the river. When I made it to the other side, I couldn't believe I had crossed the East Fork of the San Jacinto River without getting a single toe wet. From all the possible scenarios, that was the one I had least expected.

Figure 26 – Evergreen Baptist Church and San Jacinto River East Fork

Perhaps, I should have been a little disappointed to have missed out on the LSHT's biggest challenge, but I was rather thrilled that I didn't have to walk the remaining distance to Double Lake Recreation Area in soaking wet shoes and clothes. More so, since the temperature started to drop quickly as daylight faded. About two hours later, I arrived at the campground. It had already gotten dark and my legs definitely deserved some rest after the 24-mile day. I decided to just quickly eat dinner and retire into my tent early to get some extra rest, only glancing up at the night sky which was just as beautiful as the night before.

Day 5 – Double Lake Recreation Area to Tarkington (10.0 miles)

After a great night's rest, I woke up at around 7:30am to the sound of a woodpecker. When I opened my tent, I was greeted by yet another cloudless morning, and only a light wind was blowing through the tree crowns. In addition, it looked like I had the entire campground to myself. While listening to birds singing, I enjoyed an extended breakfast, sitting at a camping table, overlooking the calm surface of Double Lake. With the sun slowly rising above the tree tops, it was a particularly serene atmosphere. After breakfast, I took a luxuriously warm shower and washed off all remaining remnants of the strenuous previous day – it felt great!

Figure 27 – Double Lake Recreation Area

A short walk along the lake confirmed that Double Lake Recreation Area is definitely worth spending more time at, perhaps even an entire day. When I left the campground around noon, the weather was really warm. My feet had suffered quite a bit the day before, so I decided not to wear my hiking shoes, but instead walk in my flip-flops for a mile or two. That actually worked out so well, that I ended up leaving them on the entire day.

Not too long after leaving Double Lake, I entered the Big Creek Scenic Area. By the time a got there, quite a few day hikers had already arrived and were exploring the surroundings. Without a doubt, the protected scenic area is the most beautiful and biodiverse stretch of the LSHT. A very smooth foliage-covered path follows the meandering course of Big Creek. Little footbridges and boardwalks allow for dry crossing and add to the overall very picturesque forest setting.

Figure 28 – Hiking in Flip-Flops and Big Creek Scenic Area

There were rustling noises on both sides of the trail, but it was difficult to see anything through the thick undergrowth. I spotted a lot of squirrels, a few lizards, and many birds. The chances of seeing some of the more timid forest dwellers, such as armadillos and bobcats, can probably be increased by getting there before the crowds and also by following the side trails to the more remote corners. I definitely recommend taking your time walking through Big Creek Scenic Area and potentially combining it with a zero day at Double Lake if your schedule allows.

After leaving the protected area, the trail follows the west bank of Tarkington Bayou for almost three miles. That is another beautiful stretch which seemed to accommodate a large variety of butterflies and dragonflies. My original goal for that day was to camp at Mercy hiker camp near mile 89. When I realized I wasn't going to make it there before sunset, I decided to set up camp a few miles earlier. This would allow me to enjoy my last dinner in the forest while it was still light out. The plan worked out well because I found a perfect primitive campsite not too far from the pond at mile 85, where I had planned to resupply water for the last time anyway. The close proximity to the pond was probably the reason why I got bothered by a few mosquitoes while setting up camp. In retrospect, it is rather hard to believe that was the first time I actually noticed mosquitoes as they are typically quite bothersome on the LSHT. After dinner, I sat in front of my tent for a while to enjoy a cup of tea while reminiscing about what a great trip this had been so far. With no daylight left, I turned off my lights to enjoy the clear, starlit sky one last time.

Day 6 – Tarkington to Eastern Terminus (11.5 miles)

With less than ten miles remaining, this was going to be the most relaxed hiking day of the trip. The only time-sensitive item I had to keep an eye on was to get to Cleveland before the car rental closed at 5pm. As I was packing up my gear, I suddenly heard gunshots not too far away. Rather surprised, because theoretically hunting season was already over, I looked up to figure out what was going on. Shortly after, four men in bright orange vests carrying shotguns walked past my camp and continued on into the deeper woods without saying a word. Slightly irritated by the unexpected encounter, I finished packing up and got going.

Figure 29 – Palmetto Swamp Boardwalk and Western Ribbon Snake

The weather during the last day wasn't as great as it had been the days before. It was mostly cloudy and rather chilly, but thankfully, it wasn't raining. One of the highlights of the final stretch was a long boardwalk that took me through a rather extensive palmetto swamp. The trail was very wet and mushy in general. I noticed a lot more fallen trees in comparison to previous sections. While looking around for potential leaners, I almost didn't notice a small Western Ribbon Snake that was crossing my path. Its green and black strips blended in really well with the surrounding vegetation and underground.

Some of the footbridges along the route were slightly slanted and didn't make the steadiest impression, so once again I was very happy to have brought my trekking poles for added stability. When I finally reached the 96-mile marker, I was extremely excited and relieved at the same time. Only half a mile left to complete the longest wilderness footpath in Texas – what a great feeling! With every step that I got closer to the finish line, I felt more proud of my accomplishment, even though I have to admit that the feeling was tinged with a little sadness that this remarkable adventure would be over soon.

Figure 30 – Final Mile Marker and Eastern Terminus

When I arrived at the Winters Bayou parking lot (i.e., the Eastern Terminus of the LSHT), my adventure wasn't quite over yet. It was still about six more miles to Cleveland where my rental car was waiting for me. Since I had no desire to walk those extra miles, I had arranged for the car rental to pick me up from the parking lot. All I had to do was to give them a call and let them know I had made it there. There was only one problem, I still had no cell phone service. I walked around hoping to pick up a signal, but that was a rather fruitless endeavor. Equally unsuccessful remained my attempts to wave down a car that could give me a lift to Cleveland – I blamed it on the poor weather that day. Just as I was about to hoist my backpack once again and start walking, I ran into a friendly neighbor who let me use his home phone to get a hold of the car rental, which immediately sent a driver to pick me up. Roughly half an hour later, I was sitting in my rental car and drove to the nearest pizza place, where I devoured an entire 14-inch pizza with all the toppings civilization has to offer to celebrate my successful completion of the Lone Star Hiking Trail!

Appendices

A. Checklists

These checklists are meant to assist you with your preparations. Depending on the month you are hiking and your personal preferences, you can add or remove certain items from the lists. For those who are unsure about what to pack, if you stick to the lists, you will be in good shape.

Clothing ( ) indicates optional items

	hiking socks			light rain jacket
	underwear			hat or visor
	shorts			beanie/warm cap
	long pants (hiking or jogging)			hiking shoes
	long sleeve t-shirt (high zip collar)		( )	insect head net
	short sleeve t-shirt		( )	long underwear
	fleece jacket or sweater		( )	gloves
	warm (!) light jacket		( )	flip-flops

Personal Items (optional)

	book			notepad
	MP3 Player			pen
	mirror			

Gear ( ) indicates optional items

	backpack			extra batteries & memory card
	tent/bivy/hammock/tarp			photo ID
	sleeping bag			print-outs of all travel arrangements
	sleeping pad			map or map app
	stove			money
	fuel			shovel
	spark striker/lighter			sunglasses
	pot			toilet paper
	long spoon/utensils			towel
( )	bear canister			head lamp/solar lamp
	food			watch (rugged)
	water treatment		( )	rope
	hydration pack or bottles		( )	trekking poles
	mug (with lid)		( )	sleeping gear (ear plugs, inflatable pillow, etc.)
	pocket knife		( )	spare water reservoir (collapsible)
	first aid kit (Section 6e)		( )	medication
	silver survival blanket		( )	deodorant
	sunscreen		( )	insect repellent
( )	lip balm		( )	moisturizer
	tooth brush and paste		( )	compass
	soap (biodegradable)		( )	fishing gear
	camera		( )	GPS watch/device
( )	tripod		( )	solar charger

Food List per Day per Person (3 alternatives per meal)

Breakfast	
	2 slices of bread and peanut butter
	2 cups muesli/granola + ½ cup dried milk
	freeze dried scrambled eggs

Lunch	
	canned, dried, smoked meat + pita crisps
	fish in a pouch with 2 slices of bread
	dried hummus with 2 tortillas

Snacks	
	nuts and seeds
	dried fruit
	protein/granola bars

Dinner	
	freeze dried instant meal
	1½ cups quinoa, dried veggies + broth
	2 cups pasta, dried tomatoes + herbs

Other Food Items / Condiments

	sugar
	coffee (and creamer)
	tee (no caffeine for evenings)
	olive oil

	salt/soy sauce
	spices & herbs, hot sauce, etc.
	vitamins
	minerals

Resupply

	food
( )	sunscreen
	toilet paper
	condiments and other food items

( )	fresh fruit (e.g., apples, oranges)
( )	fresh veggies (e.g., carrots)
( )	celebratory meal (in pouch)
( )	celebratory wine (in carton)

! If you are sending your resupply with one of the major postal services, you will most probably not be allowed to send fuel. If in doubt, check their respective website.

Pre-Departure

It is recommended to go through the below list shortly before venturing onto the trail. While most of the information is available online, it is best to contact the U. S. Forest Service directly to get the latest updates. For contact information, refer to Appendix F.

	Check burn calendar for possible changes
	Check hunting calendar for possible changes
	Check weather forecast for severe conditions

	Inquire about water level at East Fork of San Jacinto River
	Inquire about general availability of water
	Inquire about possible trail section closures

B. Food Suggestions

Breakfast

- Instant oatmeal (purchase with or add flavors and sugar), porridge, semolina, and polenta with dried fruits
- Self-mixed cereals – with sesame, chia, flax, sunflower, pumpkin and other seeds; raisins and other dried fruit and berries; nuts; coconut flakes; rolled oats, shredded wheat, multi grains, etc.; mixed with dry milk, powdered soy, coconut, or almond milk, and possibly protein powder
- Pumpernickel (dark rye bread), tortilla, pita, or other dense, long-lasting breads
- Almond and peanut butter; tahini (sesame paste); chocolate spread; jelly and honey
- Freeze dried breakfasts, such as scrambled egg, hash brown, etc.
- Tea bags, tea pouches (such as ginger granulate), coffee, hot chocolate, sugar

Lunch

- Canned meat, smoked/dried sausage (e.g., traditional salami), beef and other jerkies
- Tuna and salmon in pouches; canned fish and mussels in sauces; dried salted fish and shrimp
- Hard boiled eggs (for early trail days)
- Powdered hummus (add water and olive oil)
- Crackers or pita crisps (wheat, whole grain, quinoa, corn); breads and tortillas
- Vegemite, pouches of olive oil and herbs; other veggie/vegan spreads
- Aged cheeses (repackaged in breathable material keep rather well)

Snacks

- Almonds, pistachios, other nuts and seeds (no shells, with/-out flavors, smoked)
- Dried fruits (mango, apricot, banana, date, fig, apple, etc.) and berries; fruit leather
- Power bars and gels; protein, granola, and cereal bars; other candy and snack bars
- Sundried tomatoes, veggie chips, olives in oil
- Dried corn kernels for popcorn in the evening (refine with oil, salt, sugar)
- Chocolate, gummy bears, caramel bonbons (limit these "empty calories")

Dinner

- Freeze dried instant meals in pouches (try different varieties, flavors, and brands prior)
- Pasta with sundried tomatoes, tomato paste, and/or pesto, olive oil and spices, parmesan
- Quinoa, millet, and couscous with herbs and spices (and dried carrots, onion, peas)
- Soup base or stock cubes, add noodles or rice and flakes of mushroom, parsley, tomato, etc.
- Ramen noodles and other instant dishes (e.g., macaroni & cheese, dried mashed potatoes)
- Burritos with rice, chicken in a pouch, beans, cheese, dried bell pepper
- Mixed lentils, beans, and chickpeas with seasoning (mind the cooking times)
- Condiments: salt, spices, little sachets of mustard, ketchup, hot sauce, soy sauce, olive oil
- Herbal tea, instant hot chocolate, hot lemon with honey

C. Compact Trail Guide

The compact trail guide is a comprehensive listing of LSHT trailheads, tricky waypoints, points of interest, designated hiker and hunter camps, developed campgrounds, natural and potable water sources, and trail sections where proceeding with caution is advisable.[12] For easier distinction between different trail features, the following icons are used:

TH	Trailhead	🚐	Developed campground
⛊	Tricky waypoint	◍	Natural water source
POI	Point of interest	◍	Potable water source
▲	Designated hiker or hunter camp	⚠	Proceed with caution

Mile	Icon	Trail Feature
0.0	**TH**	TH#1; Western Terminus; start of Wilderness Section (8.7 miles)
2.55	◍	Pond on right
3.5	**TH**	TH#2
3.95	◍	Low volume spring-fed creek
5.1+0.6	▲	Sand Branch Trail hiker camp
6.3	▲	Wilderness hiker camp
6.8+1.2	▲	Pole Creek Trail hiker camp
8.7	**TH**	TH#3; start of Kelly Section (7.3 miles)
9.76	◍	Pond 150 yards to the north (leave trail & follow small gully on left downstream)
11.8+0.5	▲	Caney Creek hiker camp
14.3	▲	Kelly's Pond Road hunter camp
14.3+1.2	🚐	Kelly's Pond Campground
16.0	**TH**	TH#6; start of Stubblefield Section (12.8 miles)
16.0+2.7	🚐 ◍ **POI**	Cagle Recreation Area
16.5	◍ **POI**	Great view of Lake Conroe
17.9	◍	Semi-permanent creek

---

[12] The CTG was created based on personal experience and records gathered during the author's own LSHT trip as well as information derived from LSHT Club website.

Mile	Icon	Trail Feature
19.7		Stubblefield Lake Recreation Area
20.3		Stubblefield overflow hunter camp; trail enters woods to the right (across from overflow camp), after 300 feet the trail takes a sharp left (watch as there is a trail that goes straight!)
23.5		Sharp left onto road FSR 243, then right into woods after 150 feet
24.0		Small intermittent creek (Fern Creek)
24.5		Turn right onto road FSR 243, follow for 0.2 miles, trail turns left at hikers sign
26.4		Turn right onto unmarked gravel road (Bath Ln), follow for 1.5 miles, turn right onto paved road (Ball Rd), follow for 0.15 miles, turn left onto gravel Cotton Creek Cemetery Road (past cattle guard), follow for 0.5 miles, take right fork onto unmarked road FSR 287 (past auto gate), trail enters woods on the right after 0.15 miles
28.8		Start of Huntsville Section (6.2 miles); West Huntsville hiker camp
31.1		Highest elevation (400 feet)
32.0		Turn left onto paved road, follow for a couple hundred feet until you reach small brick building (City of Huntsville Pump House, potable water tap on outside), walk towards Camelia Lake on left, cross the dam (careful, spillway can be slippery), trail turns right after dam; avoid drinking water from Camelia Lake!
33.2		Shallow spring-fed permanent creek (Alligator Creek)
35.0		TH#7; start of Phelps Section (10 miles); leave woods and turn right, walk parallel to I-45 feeder road for 0.7 miles to Park Road 40
35.7		Two options: (1) Turn left onto Park Road 40 to continue on LSHT which goes under I-45, follow for 1 mile; (2) Turn right onto Park Road 40 to enter Huntsville State Park (4.4-mile side trip)
35.7+2.2		Huntsville State Park

Mile	Icon	Trail Feature
36.7		Turn right onto US 75, follow for 0.1 mile, turn left onto Evelyn Lane, follow for 0.3 miles, trail enters woods at hiker sign on left (past blue metal gate)
38.3		Phelps hiker camp
39.3		Turn left onto Evelyn Lane (again), follow for 0.3 miles, trail enters woods at hiker sign on left
42.0		Turn left onto FM 2296, follow for 0.5 miles, turn right onto paved road (Four Notch Rd, street sign may be missing), cross railroad tracks and follow road for 2.4 miles, turn left onto FSR 213, follow for 0.1 mile to TH#8 on right
45.0		TH#8; start of Four Notch Section (9.2 miles); Four Notch hunter camp (on left)
45.3		Trail splits, follow right fork to stay on LSHT; trail on left is Four Notch Loop Trail (red markers)
48.0		Traditional halfway point of LSHT
48.2		Boswell Creek (no bridges; high-banked creek may be dangerous to cross after heavy rain)
51.3		East Four Notch hiker camp
51.5		Pond on left
51.7		Turn left onto unmarked gravel road (FSR 200), follow for 0.7 miles, turn right onto unmarked gravel road (FSR 207), follow for 0.8 miles, keep right at fork, follow FSR 207 for another mile until it intersects with FSR 202, enter woods between FSR 207 and FSR 202
54.2		Start of Big Woods Section (8.6 miles)
58.4		Trail makes sharp right turn
58.5		Off-trail pond indicated by new signage (go 300 feet east (left) of the trail down the fire break and then 100 feet south)
59.8		Trail intersects gravel road (FSR 2020D), two options: (1) turn right to continue on LSHT, enter woods after 60 feet to left; (2) turn left and walk 300 feet to get to Big Woods hiker camp
61.5		Tricky intersection with abandoned pipeline, watch for markers as trail crosses diagonally to the right!

Mile	Icon	Trail Feature
62.8	🛈 TH	TH#9; start of Magnolia Section (11 miles); turn left onto dirt road (Ira Denson Lane), follow for 0.2 miles, turn right onto John Warren Road, follow for 1.7 miles, turn left onto Hwy 150, follow for 0.3 miles to Evergreen Baptist Church (watch for flashing traffic light)
65.0	💧 🛈	Potable water tap on outside of Evergreen Baptist Church; from church, cross Hwy 150 diagonally to the left to get to FM 945, follow for 2.6 miles (mostly uphill), turn left onto S. Butch Arthur Road, TH#10 is on the corner
67.4	TH	TH#10
68.6	⛺	LSHT hiker camp #2 (tent pad + fire ring)
71.1	⚠ 💧 POI	San Jacinto River East Fork Crossing
72.2	💧	Small intermittent stream
72.8	🛈	Trail turns right (due east) along a pipeline, crosses gravel road FSR 280B, then leaves pipeline to the left (north) after 150 yards
73.8	TH	TH#11; start of Big Creek Section (8.7 miles)
75.0	🛈	Double Lake information board, two options: (1) follow LSHT which makes a U-turn around the sign; (2) follow Lake Shore Trail to the left to get to campsites
75.1	🚐 💧 POI	Double Lake Recreation Area
75.6	⛺ 🛈	LSHT hiker camp #1; cross gravel road FSR 220
78.6	🛈 POI	Go left on elevated tramway, then right back into the woods; start of Big Creek Scenic Area (2.2 miles), pay particular attention to trail markers and signs throughout the protected area as there are a number of side trails intersecting the LSHT
79.7	💧	Final crossing of Big Creek (get water here; in very dry conditions, there will be no flowing water for the next 13 miles, until you reach the San Jacinto River)
79.9	TH	TH#12
82.5	🛈 TH	TH#13; start of Tarkington Section (8.4 miles); cross the road (FM 2666) and enter the woods
83.5	🛈	Continue on LSHT or follow trail to Tarkington hunter camp on the right (1.2-mile side trip)
83.5+0.6	⛺	Tarkington hunter camp

Mile	Icon	Trail Feature
83.6	▲	Tarkington hiker camp
84.2	⑂	Trail follows west bank of Tarkington Bayou for next 2.8 miles
85.0	⬤ ⑂	Pond 150 feet on left (east) (dam visible from trail); turn left onto dirt road (pipeline), then right into woods after 150 feet
86.0	⑂	Turn left onto dirt road (FSR 2173), then right into the woods after 300 feet
86.8	⬤	Small pond on left (east)
87.0	⑂	Trail turns right leaving Tarkington Bayou, follow old tramway for 1.9 miles
88.9	⑂ ▲	Trail intersects with old logging road, two options: (1) go left to continue on LSHT; (2) walk 150 feet to the right to get to Mercy hiker camp
90.0	⑂	Cross gravel road (Forest Valley Drive)
90.9	⑂ TH	TH#14; start of Winters Bayou Section (5.6 miles); cross FM 2025, trail enters woods straight ahead
91.6	⑂	Sharp right turn, 0.1 mile straight, then sharp left turn
92.2	⚠	Very muddy area
92.5	⬤	Bridge crossing San Jacinto River East Fork
93.9	⑂	Turn right onto gravel road (FSR 274B), then left into woods after 150 feet
95.8	⬤	Iron bridge crossing Winters Bayou
96.5	TH	TH#15; Eastern Terminus

D. Example Itineraries

Below are three itinerary suggestions based on different walking speeds –
fast, moderate, and relaxed. Each itinerary proposes a suitable campsite
per day and indicates the resulting daily mileage. Be aware that none of
the itineraries include any zero days for resting or further exploration. The
three walking speeds are based on the following assumptions:

- Fast: ETD = 5; average miles per day = 19
- Moderate: ETD = 7; average miles per day = 14
- Relaxed: ETD = 10; average miles per day = 10

Destination	Mile	Fast		Moderate		Relaxed	
		day	miles	day	miles	day	miles
Western Terminus	0						
Primitive Camp*	10.0					1	10.0
Kelly's Pond HuCmp	14.3			1	14.3		
Stubblefield RecArea	19.7	1	19.7			2	9.7
W. Huntsville HiCmp	28.8			2	14.5	3	9.1
Phelps HiCmp	38.3	2	18.6			4	9.5
Four Notch HuCmp	45.0			3	16.2		
E. Four Notch HiCmp	51.3					5	13.0
Big Woods HiCmp	59.8	3	21.5	4	14.8	6	8.5
LSHT hiker camp #2	68.6					7	8.8
Double Lake RecArea	75.1			5	15.3	8	6.5
Tarkington HiCmp	83.6	4	23.8				
Mercy HiCmp	88.9			6	13.8	9	13.8
Eastern Terminus	96.5	5	12.9	7	7.6	10	7.6

*Primitive camping is restricted during hunting season!

E. Side Trails

Below is a list of LSHT side trails. For each trail, it is noted at which mile(s) (west-to-east) it intersects with the LSHT. The table also includes corresponding trail marker colors and trail lengths.

Note: In order to determine the length of the full loop for a particular side trail, calculate the distance between the side trail's 1st and 2nd intersection with the LSHT and add it to the length noted in the table!

1st Intersect. (LSHT mile)	Trail Name	Marker Color	Length (miles)	2nd Intersect. (LSHT mile)
0.1	Little Lake Creek Loop Trail (LLCLT)	Orange-silver	17.7	11.8
3.3	West Fork Trail	Blue-silver	0.3*	via LLCLT
3.7	North Wilderness Trail	Red-silver	2.2	8.0
5.1	Sand Branch Trail	Yellow-silver	0.7*	via LLCLT
6.8	Pole Creek Trail	Blue-silver	1.2*	via LLCLT
45.3	Four Notch Loop Trail	Red-silver	4.9	49.3
74.9	Double Lake Trail**	n/a	4.8	75.1
79.1	Big Creek Trail	Orange-silver	0.6	80.1
79.2	White Oak Trail	Green-silver	0.5	80.1
79.5	Pine Trail	Yellow-silver	0.2	79.8

*Distance to Little Lake Creek Loop Trail

**Double Lake Rec. Area offers a number of additional trails to further explore the area

F. Contact Information

Double Lake Recreation Area
301 FM 2025
Coldspring, TX 77331
Phone: 1 (936) 653-3448

Huntsville State Park
565 Park Road 40 West
Huntsville, TX 77340
Phone: 1 (936) 295-5644

Lone Star Hiking Trail Club, Inc.
113 Ben Drive
Houston, TX 77022
Email: trailguide@lonestartrail.org

Sam Houston National Forest (U. S. Forest Service)
394 FM 1375 West
New Waverly, TX 77358
Phone: 1 (936) 344-6205
Toll free: 1 (888) 361-6908
Fax: 1 (936) 344-2123

G. Links & References

Houston Wilderness

Detailed information about the Piney Woods:

http://houstonwilderness.org/piney-woods/

Lake Conroe Texas

Brief history & photos of Lake Conroe:

http://www.lakeconroe.com/about-lake-conroe/

Lone Star Hiking Trail Club

Current information on LSHT conditions & events as well as trail maps:

http://www.lonestartrail.org

Recreational Equipment, Inc. (REI)

Wide-ranging outdoor advice & products:

http://www.rei.com/learn/expert-advice.html

Somers, Karen

Detailed description of the LSHT's history & wildlife as well as its trail sections:

The Lone Star Hiking Trail: The official guide to the longest wilderness footpath in Texas, Wilderness Press, 2009

StateImpact Texas

Information about the top ten invasive species in Texas:

http://stateimpact.npr.org/texas/2012/04/13/the-top-ten-invasive-species-in-texas/

Texas Department of State Health Services

A guide to the treatment of victims envenomed by snakes and spiders native to Texas:

https://www.dshs.state.tx.us/idcu/health/zoonosis/animal/bites/infor mation/venom/

Texas Parks & Wildlife

Overview of outdoor activity regulations in Sam Houston National Forest (incl. hiking, camping, hunting, fishing):

https://tpwd.texas.gov/huntwild/hunt/wma/find_a_wma/list/?id=30

Detailed description of Huntsville State Park:

http://tpwd.texas.gov/state-parks/huntsville

Wildlife fact sheets:

https://tpwd.texas.gov/huntwild/wild/species/

U. S. Forest Service (United States Department of Agriculture)

Detailed information about the Sam Houston National Forest:

http://www.fs.usda.gov/detail/texas/about-forest/districts/?cid= fswdev3_008443

Forest maps with hunter camp locations:

http://www.fs.usda.gov/detail/texas/maps-pubs/?cid=FSWDEV3_ 008434

And, of course, visit

www.PlanAndGoHiking.com

for more information, pictures, and posts.

We look forward to and appreciate your feedback!

H. List of Abbreviations

BCSA	Big Creek Scenic Area
DLRA	Double Lake Recreation Area
CTG	Compact Trail Guide
ETD	Estimate of Trail Days
FM	Farm-to-Market Road
FSR	Forest Service Road
HVSP	Huntsville State Park
LLCLT	Little Lake Creek Loop Trail
LSHT	Lone Star Hiking Trail
POI	Point of Interest
RA	Recreation Area
SA	Scenic Area
SHNF	Sam Houston National Forest
SP	State Park
USFS	United States Forest Service

I. LSHT Club

The Lone Star Hiking Trail Club, Inc., a 501(c)(3) nonprofit organization, was formed in 1995 on National Trails Day and is affiliated with the American Hiking Society. Their mission is (1) to educate the public about location, use and needs of the hiking trails of Texas, with emphasis on the Lone Star Hiking Trail, and (2) to provide volunteer assistance for maintenance and improvement of hiking trails. The club name reflects their emphasis on the Lone Star Hiking Trail and their Texas location.

The Lone Star Hiking Trail Club hosts events all year round. Experienced volunteer leaders guide group hikes and trail maintenance hikes on the 2nd and 4th Saturday of each month. The LSHT Club is funded through donations and annual membership contributions (currently $20.00/year for adults). Event locations are primarily on the Lone Star Hiking Trail in the Sam Houston National Forest.

More information is available online at *http://www.lonestartrail.org* or can be requested via email at *trailguide@lonestartrail.org*.

About the Author

Kevin is a seasoned backpacker who was first introduced to the fascinating world of hiking by his parents during family vacations in the beautiful Czech Giant Mountains and Saxon Elbe Sandstone Mountains in Europe. Inspired by those early adventures, Kevin went on to travel and explore Europe's largest mountain range, the Alps, on foot and on skis throughout the years. In 2011, he moved to San Diego, California, which quickly became his gateway to the Golden State's vast and varied backcountry.

Together with family and friends or solo, Kevin has since embarked on many backpacking adventures and multi-day trips in state parks, national forests, and of course the Sierra Nevada mountains. With a degree in business and IT, he is not only fascinated by the physical and mental challenges arising from hiking long distances, but also by streamlining all aspects of the planning process and trying out new advances in gear. To Kevin, hiking is a great way to escape the comfort zone and reconnect with nature while exploring remote and pristine corners of the world that are solely accessible on foot.

Special Thanks

I would like to extend a special thank you to:

My family, in particular my parents, who sparked my interest for the great outdoors early on. During countless excursions, near and far, they shared their knowledge and appreciation of nature, which ultimately motivated me to keep exploring and venture off on my own. Furthermore, their trust and hands-off approach have taught me a good amount of autonomy and common sense, two indispensable skills not only for everyday life, but also for spending extended periods of time in remote wilderness.

My friend and fellow traveler Gerret, who shares the same appreciation of nature and enthusiasm when it comes to planning outdoor expeditions. His particular passion for hiking has brought forth one of the most practical and motivating guidebooks on hiking the John Muir Trail in California and inspired a fruitful collaboration, which led to the creation of this book. I am very grateful for our exceptional friendship.

My friend Thomas and his wife Lovisa, who warmly welcomed me into their home after my hike and spared no effort to give me an excellent tour of Houston and surroundings. They also introduced me to the many culinary specialties East Texas has to offer.

Disclaimer

The information provided in this book is accurate to the best of the authors' and publisher's knowledge. However, there is no aspiration, guarantee, or claim to the correctness, completeness, and validity of any information given. Readers should be aware that internet addresses, phone numbers, mailing addresses, as well as prices, services, etc. were believed to be accurate at time of publication, but are subject to change without notice.

References are provided for informational purposes only. Neither authors nor the publisher have control over the content of websites, books, or other third party sources listed in this book and, consequently, do not accept responsibility for any content referred to herein. The mention of companies, organizations, or authorities in this book does not imply endorsement by author(s) or publisher, and vice versa.

This book is not a medical guidebook. The information and advice provided herein are merely intended as reference and explicitly not as a substitute for professional medical advice. Consult a physician to discuss whether or not your health and fitness level are appropriate for the physical activities describe in this book; especially, if you are aware of any preexisting conditions or issues.

60757772R00082

Made in the USA
Lexington, KY
17 February 2017